The Silent Minority

The Silent Minority

Children with disabilities in Asian families

Robina Shah

ISBN 1 874 579 44 X

Revised edition published by National Children's Bureau Enterprises Ltd
8 Wakley Street
London EC1V 7QE

National Children's Bureau Enterprises Ltd is the trading company of the National Children's Bureau (Registered Charity no. 258825).

Typeset, printed and bound in the European Union by Saxon Graphics Ltd, Derby.

The National Children's Bureau was established as a registered charity in 1963. Our purpose is to identify and promote the interests of all children and young people and to improve their status in a diverse society.

We work closely with professionals and policy makers to improve the lives of all children but especially young children, those affected by family instability, children with special needs or disabilities and those suffering the effects of poverty and deprivation.

We collect and disseminate information about children and promote good practice in children's services through research, policy and practice development, publications, seminars, training and an extensive library and information service.

The Bureau works in partnership with Children in Scotland and Children in Wales.

Contents

Acknowledgements

Responsibility for the text of this book is entirely my own and the views expressed do not necessarily represent those of the National Children's Bureau. But the book could not have been produced without the help of many individuals and organisations.

I would like to acknowledge my thanks to Manchester and Birmingham Social Services, in particular Mike Kavanagh, without whose input this study could not have been initiated.

My thanks also go out to Manchester Council for Community Relations for allocating special time so that the research could be completed. Furthermore, my grateful thanks to Professor Sainsbury and the Joseph Rowntree Trust for their assistance throughout the writing up of the book.

In addition, I would like to say thank you to all the parents, social workers, typist Lynn Sutton and many others who have supported and helped me in both finding the material and conducting the research.

My grateful thanks go to Philippa Russell of the Council for Disabled Children, for her advice and to Fiona Blakemore and the National Children's Bureau for wishing to publish my book.

Last but not least my special thanks go to my parents, my daughter Zainab and my husband who gave me the confidence and will to write about my feelings on this hugely unrepresented area and to realise an ambition.

Glossary

This set of terms will appear throughout this book and so I have chosen to provide the reader with definitions to avoid any confusion.

Asian

This refers to persons or descendants from the Indian sub-continent and persons who identify themselves as being Asian within this context. In Britain, this generally refers to Pakistani, India, Sikh, Bangladeshi and Gujeratis. This may also include Asians who have come to Britain via East Africa or other countries. In this instance Vietnamese, Chinese and people from the Far East are not included in this definition.

Black

This term reflects the power division between White and non-White and therefore refers to any non-White person. Black is often used a political term although its application as an identity tag varies according to experience, consciousness and context.

Social worker

Although this study was concerned principally with the social workers from the local authority, I have used the term to include other professionals from the caring services and therefore lower case letters are used rather than capitals, to indicate the broad areas within social work.

Use of disability/handicap

Readers will note that 'disability' and 'handicap' are used interchangeably in different sections of this book. Many Asian families still prefer or understand the term 'handicap' in preference to 'disability' and we have therefore reflected the dual use of these definitions in the text.

Foreword

Over the past decade, there has been increasing awareness of the importance of listening to the views of parents of children with disabilities and of planning services which are sensitive to individual family needs. But there has also been corresponding concern about the stereotypes which have been created around the feelings and perceptions of *Asian* families about the level and nature of support which they would welcome within their local communities. Listening to parents has never been easy. It challenges both professionals and service systems. It can be both painful and time-consuming. But there is growing evidence that the spirit of the Children Act – partnership with parents and children – is possible and that parents are indeed the most effective carers and educators of their children, provided that they receive appropriate guidance and support to fulfil these roles.

The Children Act has also introduced a new and timely duty, namely the requirement that local authorities should ensure that the planning, provision and publicity relating to family support services should reflect the religions, cultures, ethnicity and languages of the communities they serve. Four years ago the Council for Disabled Children was privileged to work with the Department of Health and with representatives of the Asian Community in producing a video and support materials on the theme of *Physical and Mental Handicap in the Asian Community: Can My Child be Helped?* This project demonstrated the double jeopardy of many Asian families with children with special needs. Services were frequently not available in the relevant language or else were inappropriate to the families' cultural or religious needs. Parents were also not offered services, on the assumption that they would not wish to utilise respite care or other support services because care would be within the extended family alone. Robina Shah has herself noted that:

> 'Disability of whatever kind does not discriminate. It transcends all races, beliefs and cultures. It creates similarly profound emotional, practical and psychological experiences for all parents, wherever they are. Unfortunately, where families from minority ethnic groups are concerned, common sense about valid generalisations of attitudes towards disability is lost in the mists of ignorance and perceived cultural differences.'

The Silent Minority is an important milestone in helping all of us to understand the feelings and wishes of Asian families and to appreciate how easily services may appear negative, when barriers of language and culture are not seriously addressed. Most importantly it helps us to begin to share and to understand the values and beliefs which are part of the Asian community and which underpin their family lives and the care they wish to secure for their children.

The book also underlines the isolation, grief and anxiety which *all* families with disabled children experience as they come to terms with the multiplicity of demands, wide range of service providers and worries that accompany diagnosis of a disability or special need. But it also makes clear recommendations for achieving integration and positive partnerships between Asian children, families and their local communities which is achievable if we see the world and services provided through the *families'* eyes.

Robina Shah's book reinforces the key messages of the Children Act. Practical, sensitive and challenging, it fills an important gap in the extensive literature about families of children with special needs, their wishes and aspirations and their capacity to cope with appropriate support. It also reminds us that in an increasingly diverse society, we need to constantly inform professional practice about the impact of culture, ethnicity and religion on the needs of all families, particularly those caring for children with disabilities and special needs.

The Silent Minority also has important messages for child health services. Purchasers and providers of health care will find useful guidance on how to ensure that Asian families use the full range of services available to the general population and what special factors should be considered in order to create user-friendly services for children with disabilities and special needs and their families within the Asian community. Robina Shah highlights the importance of good quality community services, the need to develop access arrangements for families from minority ethnic groups and the lessons that can be learned from developing services in full consultation with all sectors of local communities.

Recent changes in the education system, in particular Part III of the 1993 Education Act and the *Code of Practice on Identification and Assessment of Special Educational Needs* (DFE, 1994) have also highlighted the need to encourage parents to be directly involved in assessment, intervention and review of their children's special educational needs. The concept of 'partnership with parents' has been a cornerstone of special educational needs provision since the 1978 Warnock Report. It is also a key principle within the new guidance on community child health services, which reflects the Health of the Nation targets, which in turn expect that quality standards for purchasers and providers of health care should demonstrate consultation with minority ethnic communities. But partnership is challenging, can be problematic, and requires genuine commitment by all concerned. *The Silent Minority* reminds us of the importance of ensuring 'equal access to information and services' and in particular of acknowledging that we all 'need to change services so that they reflect a diversity of needs; avoid stereotypes and engage local communities in change and development'. Robina Shah offers many positive and practical recommendations for ensuring that Asian families with disabled children are *not* silent minorities and that their wishes and needs are fully incorporated into wider strategic planning within local communities.

Philippa Russell

Preface

On completion of my training as a psychologist in 1985 I decided to work in Community Relations. During my first six months I spent time working with White professionals in the statutory and non-statutory services who had some contact with Black clients. On one of these visits, I attended a summer playscheme in Cheetham Hill, Manchester.

While enjoying the happy atmosphere the children on the playscheme had created, I focused on two Pakistani children who were obviously not participating in the fun. At that time, I was not close enough to them to understand that the reason for their non-participation was because they were both severely mentally handicapped and confined to wheelchairs. I felt an obligation to obtain a greater insight into their lives; to find out how their parents were coping, what services were available, and how the parents responded to services offered and whether they felt they were appropriate. Question after question surfaced and I approached somebody who had been working with these children and their families. After a half-hour discussion it was confirmed that very little information existed on the needs of local Asian families who had children with learning difficulties. There was very little support either within social services or within the community in this area and the main problem was that the perceived need, based on minimal information, obscured the 'real need'.

In the months following this visit I began to formulate a questionnaire, see Appendix 1, based on conversations with social workers and health professionals working in the area of learning difficulties. I knew that I must ensure that parental needs were given a high profile as the only means available to assess the validity of services in terms of appropriateness and sensitivity. The main theme running through my discussions with workers in the caring professions was centred around their lack of understanding of the Asian community and their dependence on stereotypes to offer them some type of blueprint to work from – even though they acknowledged that the stereotypes are wrong.

The next task was to contact families. The best way of doing this, I thought, was to get in touch with established self-help groups in Manchester for parents of children with learning difficulties. I wrote several letters to local voluntary organisations only to receive letters of apology saying that they were very sorry but they had no Asian or, for that matter, Black members. I was concerned that self-help groups and statutory services had been unsuccessful in recruiting membership from the Asian community. I was not convinced that there was a real commitment to ensuring that these families were aware of voluntary organisations that might help them. It was acknowledged that children with learning difficulties were living in Asian families but if Asian parents did not contact such groups themselves, this was felt to be indicative of their wish to remain separate and isolated from White-based organisations and services. In other words, the onus of responsibility was placed solely on the Asian parents. The questions of the cultural barrier, lack of information and inaccessibility were seen as irrelevant – after all, there are many White parents who choose to be left alone and nobody enquires about them, do they?

It appeared that the only resource was to contact Asian parents through their social workers. In the north of Manchester in 1986, out of a possible 300 registered families only 12 were Asian clients who had severe learning difficulties. Eventually, I interviewed these families and their responses were recorded in a short report entitled 'Attitudes, services and stereotypes and the Asian disabled client' which was published in *Community Care* in May 1987. The report received a huge reaction and, over a period of three months, I was inundated with requests for copies of the full report and further information. I now had two incentives to conduct further investigations in this important area of concern: the first was my increasing desire to redress the balance of services to a client group whose need for help had too often been ignored or misunderstood. Secondly, there was a tremendous amount of genuine interest shown by White practitioners in obtaining more support and information about the

Asian community and disability. Here, I would be providing assistance not only to parents but also to their providers, and it was very rewarding to be given the opportunity to address at least some of the problems encountered by both provider and client groups. Here I had the chance to share my professional experience, an experience channelled through my own cultural and racial identity, which has enabled me to gain a greater understanding about Asian parents and their cultural, religious, social welfare and health needs.

With the help of The Joseph Rowntree Foundation, I was able to carry out further interviews, which included families from Birmingham, and in 1988 the findings of my research were written up in the form of a book. I wanted the book to highlight the problems faced by parents and workers but I did not want to leave the reader without any means to challenge them, and to improve attitudes and service provision to Asian parents with learning difficulties. If the reader begins to have a better understanding of the wide and varying needs of the Asian community, on an objective level which endorses individuality and dilutes generality, then this book will have served its purpose. A conscious decision was taken not to write in 'textbook language' because I want this book to be enjoyed by the reader as an informative, educational and a positive resource, and, through that stimulation, to shake the conscience and motivate a challenge to good practice.

This book is not a comprehensive account of the situation of Asian families where one or more of the children are mentally or physically disabled but rather an attempt to promote increased awareness of some of the difficulties such families encounter during their everyday lives, with particular reference to their contacts with social services. The aim of the book is:

- to challenge some of the stereotypes held by social workers, and others about Asian parents' attitudes towards their disabled child;
- to give a brief insight into how Asian parents perceive the role of the social worker in meeting the needs of their disabled child;
- to investigate Asian parents' knowledge of the services available and, more importantly, their feelings about the appropriateness of these services;

- to put forward recommendations in the light of the Children Act 1989 and the NHS and Community Care Act 1990, which will prioritise areas of concern and facilitate the implementation of a more accessible, appropriate and effective service delivery to Asian families with a disabled child.

The most important message from my research is to listen to and learn from the parents of children with disabilities. In this book I explore the additional special needs of Asian families who are living with disability and I identify a number of strategies for offering advice and support which is sensitive and appropriate to their culture and needs.

One Asian parent of a child with a disability speaks:

'I was sixteen when I married, I came to this strange country knowing no-one except my husband. All of my relatives were in Pakistan. When my child was born he was normal and I was the happiest mother on earth. Then two years later he got meningitis; he was very ill and I thought he was going to die. In fact I wished he had died when the doctor told me that he was severely mentally handicapped. Nineteen-years-old and my whole world had collapsed; I wanted to run but there was no-one to run to. My husband felt the pain but we were both too hurt to comfort each other. One evening he spent the whole night crying; he sounded just like a small child.

Our son is now seven, we both love him very much. It took some time to cope and I didn't quite understand how to at first, but when there is no-one else but yourself, you learn to rely on each other and cope.'

Introduction

When discussing service provision to the Asian community it appears that this often involves a homogeneous response based on an over-generalisation and over-simplification of their social welfare needs. In order to challenge this process the first chapter in this book will address the assumption of homogeneity and will look at how the Asian community is made up of groups with various, and extremely distinctive, individual, cultural, religious, linguistic and social values. In terms of addressing the needs of the Asian disabled client, local authorities are shown to be currently unable to provide an 'acceptable service'. Attaching responsibility for difficulties to the individual or the culture of origin is a commonly used form of social control, and means that the 'solutions' to the 'problems' may be couched in the context of individual action without involving financial expenditure or changes in social and economic structures. Social services can be used in this way, where an inadequacy in services is attributed to cultural or religious practices among the clients.

There is a risk that concentrating interest on the specific cultural mores of a particular ethnic group may have the effect of identifying some groups of people as 'problems'. This in itself tends to obscure the role of institutional racism and the actions of the community which are active in the reinforcement of the viewpoint that 'It's not the services which are inadequate, it's the people'. Although many local authorities are aware of the need to redress the imbalance of services to Asian people with disabilities, there is little existing information to provide them with details about how a more equitable service may be achieved. It is within this context that the research documented in this book was conducted.

The main area of concern was to dispel the stereotypical views that non-Asian social workers had of the Asian community and their attitudes towards disability. By providing an insight into the perceived and felt needs of the Asian disabled client it is hoped that a more sensitive understanding of the issues related to disability will be reached, which will be instrumental in creating increased awareness of individual requirements in the provision of specialist care.

The families were selected by contacting Manchester and Birmingham Social Services Departments, and both departments were instrumental in contacting the families and requesting their permission to be interviewed for this research. My thanks go to all the people involved in this process, without whose help the research could not have taken place.

The research

The subjects for the study were Asian parents who had children aged up to 19 years with severe learning difficulties. In Manchester and Birmingham the families were contacted through social services and special schools respectively. Letters were sent to the parents about the prospective study, requesting their permission for the author to contact them directly. Once permission was received the author wrote to the parents individually and a time was arranged for interviews to take place. A questionnaire and semi-structured interview was used. In the majority of cases the interviews were conducted in the language of the subjects' choice, mostly Urdu or Punjabi, and interpreters were not required as the author is fluent in both languages. Fourteen families were interviewed in Birmingham over a period of three days and 21 in Manchester over a period of two weeks, with each interview lasting approximately an hour.

The questionnaire was divided into four sections:

- attitudes of parent to child;
- attitudes of parent to social worker;
- knowledge of services;
- general issues of family experience and family functioning.

Responses to the questionnaire were recorded and are set out in tables in Appendix 1. Case studies for each family were also recorded and have been used throughout the book, while others may be referred to in Appendix 2.

The results

The findings of the study suggest that attitudes based on stereotypes about the attitudes and needs of Asian families in general were often demonstrated by social workers when determining the needs of a specific Asian family and its disabled child.

Conclusion

In order to counter this problem, the report concludes, it is essential that the attitudes of services and social workers become more sensitive to the cultural and religious perspectives of the Asian client with a disability. Through a comprehensive list of recommendations in Chapter 6, the author attempts to highlight key areas where change in attitude and service delivery can best be achieved.

The book

In writing up the findings of this research I have chosen to do so under specific chapter headings. This I feel will be more beneficial to the reader than a more general survey based on standard research-type protocol. Each type heading corresponds to a section within the interview schedule. All information included will be indicative of the respondents' answers. Each chapter concludes with a 'Signpost' which is a brief summary of the main points of the chapter.

1. Setting the context

Reference has been made to a tendency to use the word 'Asian' to denote a 'homogeneous' group. Such a classification encourages generalisations leading to inaccurate, inappropriate and insensitive summations of an individual Asian client's needs and experiences. 'Asian' refers to a number of groups originating from the Indian subcontinent, China, Malaysia, the Soviet Union, and so on. However, in this book the term 'Asian' will refer to those persons originating from the Indian sub-continent (see Fig. 1). Even within this limitation, the term 'Asian' still represents many variations of habitat, religion and language. It must also be remembered that there are a number of people who refer to themselves as Asian, even though they have been born in Britain – the increasing Asian second generation. Problems of communication may arise, for example when fiancés/fiancées arrive in the UK to join their spouses, in addition to the obvious cultural, linguistic, social and economic inequalities that may exist.

Generalisations about the cultural, social and religious back-grounds of Asian minority groups can be very misleading, and it is important for social workers to have an understanding of each group's religious, cultural and social composition. Furthermore, as in most countries, Asian people vary considerably in their personal convictions and life styles, and it is essential to remember that the extent to which individuals observe their religious and cultural mores also varies greatly. In addition, many Asians have modified their attitudes to diet, religious observances and dress since coming to the UK. Within an Asian family, the extent of modification may vary – between the generations, and between men and women. This chapter is intended to be used as a general guide rather than a strict

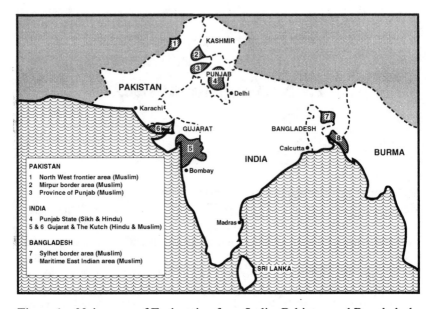

Figure 1   Main areas of Emigration from India, Pakistan and Bangladesh

interpretation. Emphasis is placed on describing religious and cultural backgrounds as these are the areas where misinterpretations are most frequently made. However, in order to have a greater understanding of the Asian community, an important prerequisite is to understand the prevalence of racism and the historical roots from which it grew.

A brief examination of the history of racism

The history of British imperialism and legislation constraining immigration forms the basis from which contemporary race relations take their shape. The role of the British Empire has been well documented, as have the effects of imperialism on individuals and, although it is not the purpose here to cover these in detail, their general influences must be taken into account. Britain's imperialist history has an impact on both Black and White people today through its legacy of economic imbalances, unequal power relations and images of the colonised and the colonisers. The slavery of the seventeenth, eighteenth and nineteenth centuries, although not principally accountable for racism, did give rise to the notion that Black people, who were bought and sold like cattle, were unable to be anything other than inferior to the White middle classes who owned them. Furthermore, since most slaves were Black, the colour of their skins became synonymous with negative attitudes about their race.

During the Victorian era an attitude of inferiority towards Black people was fostered: the world was seen as being in racial strata, with White men holding the reins and promoting the perceived superiority of their civilisation. Even today this attitude holds sway; Black people are less frequently in positions of management and, in spite of equal opportunities legislation and attempts at positive action, Black people are still over-represented in the lower socio-economic groups.

Armed with the notion that White supremacy was inevitable in the world, when Victorian settlers began to expand into Africa and India they considered the cultures they observed to be heathen, barbaric and uncivilised. These views also provided a useful *post hoc* rationalisation for the development of trade based on the exploitation of natural resources. Thus, the empire builders set out to 'civilise' the Black races; to persuade them that their way of life was valueless and without higher purpose, and that they should therefore accept and appreciate the 'good standard of life' that White people were able to give them.

In the creation of the British Raj on the Indian subcontinent wars were fought and won by the British. As a result of the East India Shipping Company trading in a country with enormous wealth-creating potential, the British Army was sent to India to support British interests against the opposition of the French, Dutch and Portuguese who were also eager to increase their access to foreign wealth. After the army came the civil service and the missionaries, and the Indian people soon found themselves defenceless against the British colonialists whom they had warmly welcomed into their country, unaware of the lives and wealth they were to lose as a result. Although many of the British who lived there came to love and respect India, they failed to realise that this established and flourishing country was, in effect, the victim of their occupancy. Alongside extensive exploitation was the insensitivity to a culture which had been highly developed.

Migration to the mother country

What then is the heritage of attitudes in Britain towards the new settlers who came to find employment and a new life in their 'mother country', following the Second World War? Migration between countries and continents has been part of the world's development for centuries and, just as a century or two ago the British felt 'justified' in infiltrating their culture across the continents, so it can be argued that migration from the so-called New Commonwealth is really a consequence of early colonisation.

The need for post-war reconstruction and the expansion of the Western European economies heralded migration to the mother country. These factors coupled with a fall in the economically active population – because of death or injury in the war, and an increase in the number of old and the retired – created a shortage of labour in western Europe and migrant labour was needed. A recruiting campaign was initiated and workers were recruited not only from Britain's traditional source, Ireland, but also from another source, the residue of the dying British Empire – particularly the Caribbean, India, Bangladesh and Pakistan. London Transport sent out its recruiting officers to Jamaica; Bradford Mill owners sent out their scouts to Kashmir, Pakistan and India, again asking people to come and fill a severe labour shortage – 'to come and work their passage to British citizenship'. In effect, they were coming to do the jobs left vacant arguably because British White people didn't want to do them: for example, certain dirty jobs with night-shifts, low pay and poor working conditions; unskilled jobs in cotton mills and textile industries – heavy industries which had boomed in Victorian times but were in decline in the later twentieth century. It is ironic that now, in a period of growing technology, it is the Pakistani innovative entrepreneur who has brought the textile industries of the North back into prominence.

This chain of migration brought many difficulties for the immigrants who arrived to find themselves perceived as 'dirty', 'Pakis', 'coons' and 'wogs'. They could not understand why the White residents of the mother country were so hostile and arrogant towards them; after all, they had invited them to come and work in their country, so why were they now so inconsiderate and racist? With the steady influx of Black immigrants, White Britons relatively quickly came into personal contact with various unknown cultures and languages: everything was different about the immigrants – the way they dressed, cooked and consumed their food, the way they talked and worked. Such differences were regarded as a negative invasion and there were heated debates about segregation and separation to protect the indigenous society from being overwhelmed by an immigrant race and culture. In an attempt to control this extreme response various means were used to encourage White Britons to accept the new immigrants. So the notion of assimilation was born: 'become like us and racism will be reduced; wear my clothes and think like I do and I will forget you are Black'. However, assimilation was not the answer, and can never be so. Britain is now a multiracial, multicultural society, and Black people are fighting to maintain the richness of their cultures and religions – still struggling, as they did when they first arrived, to keep their identities.

In Britain the images of past imperialism and the unequal present remain. Legislation has virtually put a stop to new immigration and has yet to tackle effectively the racial discrimination that pervades all aspects of British life, and which influences individual behaviour and responses, whether unconsciously or consciously. Policies have changed from a concern that Black people should be assimilated into the majority White society to multiculturalism, which propounds the view that all cultures should be retained on an equal basis. Below the surface, however, the policies have changed little and racism continues to be largely unchallenged. Black people continue to be discriminated against, in housing, employment, health provisions, the legal system, education and immigration; blame is attached to them as 'social problems' rather than to the White racism which keeps their social status low. Until White society re-educates itself and moves away from the negative attitudes fostered during the colonial years, racism will continue and any challenge to it will be unsuccessful.

A prerequisite for counteracting racism is greater understanding; first of one's own attitudes, and second of the various and individual groups of Black people. Black and Asian people are not an homogeneous group but represent wide cultural, religious and linguistic diversity.

The Asian community – who are they?

A knowledge of peoples' value systems, which may be different to one's own because of cultural and religious mores, is relevant to the findings of the present study. Furthermore, it can teach us something about ourselves as individuals, especially in broadening our appreciation of just how diverse the Asian community is. Within the large Asian population (as defined within this study) currently living in Britain, the major groups come from east or west Punjab in Pakistan and India. These are either Sikhs or Muslims. Others come from Bengal, particularly around Sylhet and are also Muslims. The people from the Gujerat, on the west coast of India, are largely Hindu, though with a substantial proportion of Muslims. East African Asians are mostly Gujerati or Sikhs. It is now appropriate to consider their separate identities and cultural/religious differences.

Islam

In Pakistan, Islam is the state religion, but Muslims also form 10 per cent of the total population of India and 90% of the population in Bangladesh. In England, Muslims form over 35 per cent of the total Asian population and are from Pakistan, Bangladesh, Kashmir (Mirpur) and Gujerat. Islam is a world religion, of course, practised in the Middle East (Yemen, Gulf States, Saudi Arabia, Iran, Iraq and North Africa) and thus many of the points considered here are equally relevant and appropriate to these groups.

To a Muslim, Islam is a way of life governing not only religious practice and morality, but social patterns, marriage, divorce, kinship, and economic and political relationships. There are five essential religious duties for a Muslim and they are often referred to as the five pillars of Islam:

- The declaration of faith – there is no deity except Allah (God) and Muhammad is his last prophet.
- The duty to offer five daily prayers at appointed times.
- The requirement of Zakat, which is compulsory alms-giving to the poor (two and a half per cent per annum of a man's accumulated wealth).
- The obligation to fast during the month of Ramadan.
- The duty to undertake the Haj – to make the pilgrimage to Mecca.

There are common scriptural and historical roots for both Christianity and Judaism. The brotherhood of man within the faith is emphasised and the concept of caste rejected: in Islam all men are equal. Muslims believe that the Holy *Quran*, revealed through the

Prophet Muhammad, is the true word of God and contains his final revelations for the guidance of mankind.

Unlike other religions Islam lays down a detailed code of conduct for day-to-day life and social affairs, known as the Shariah or Islamic law. The Shariah is integral to the social, political and cultural life of Muslims. The prayers, five times a day, are associated with purification and washing rituals as a necessary preparation. Muslims attach great importance to cleanliness, and hands, feet and mouth are always washed before prayers. Midday prayers for males on Friday must be said in a group while other prayers may be said individually. Similarly there are regulations affecting social behaviour, including rules concerning marriage, inheritance and diet. By Muslim dietary law alcohol is forbidden and no pork may be eaten. Similarly, animals for eating must be slaughtered in a particular religious way, the meat then being called Halal, meaning lawful; that which is unlawful is called Haram.

The Muslim family is usually an extended family with different relations having varying responsibilities. Islam affirms the equality of men and women as human beings, although rules for men and women are different and the free mixing of the two sexes is disapproved of. Traditionally women should cover their heads and bodies and avoid social contact with unrelated men. Broadly speaking this practice is called 'Purdah' or veiling. Islam enjoins marriage and, although misconceptions are common in the UK about polygamy among Muslims, in practice Muslims in this country have only one wife. In Pakistan it is possible to have more than one wife but there are certain conditions attached this: the permission of the first wife is essential, and there must be strong reasons for the husband to justify the need for a second wife – for example, if the first wife is unable to bear children. It should be stressed that, even though these observances are strictly prescribed for Muslims, there are regional and cultural differences in the importance of particular observances for individuals or groups.

Important Islamic festivals

These festivals are dictated by the lunar calendar and are normally not fixed until, at most, four to six weeks before the event. In Islamic states all festivals are public holidays. Those marked with an asterisk are ones which only some Muslims may wish to take as holidays.

Eid-ul-Fitr* This is celebrated at the end of the fasting month, Ramadan. Feasting is followed by the visiting of relatives and friends. Here the wearing of new clothes forms a significant part of the festival, as does the giving of presents and money to the younger members in the family.

Eid-ul-Adha This festival is celebrated on the tenth day of the Islamic calendar month of Zhul-Haj, and marks the annual completion of the Hijra pilgrimage to Mecca. During this time Muslims all over the world offer sacrifices of lamb, goat, cow or camel, in commemoration of the prophet Abraham's sacrifice at God's command. The meat is then distributed among the poor.

Muharram* The commencement of the Islamic year, this is the anniversary of the Hijra or migration of the prophet Muhammad from Mecca to Medina in 622 AD, where he and his companions organised the first Muslim community. Some Muslims fast during this time.

Tenth of Muharram* Muslims commemorate the martyrdom of Imam Hussain, grandson of the prophet Muhammad.

Ramadan Ramadan is an obligatory month of fasting (30 days) when all Muslims are expected to abstain from all food, drink and tobacco from dawn to dusk, with the exception of the ill, pregnant women and young children. The fasting celebrates the sending down of the *Quran* as a guide for all mankind and teaches the value of self-discipline.

Eid festivals are probably the most important times when Muslims would wish to have time off from work, not merely for time to be spent in prayer, but also for the preparation for the festival, and the greetings and meals which follow it. In addition, certain aspects of the Islamic faith such as corporate prayers on Fridays, may lead to requests for time off and the provision of prayer rooms.

Sikhism

In India this is a strong and significant reformist sect based in the Punjab (under 5 per cent of the total population of India). Sikhs are the largest religious group of Indians to have emigrated to England, comprising 50 per cent of the Asian population.

Sikhism developed in the sixteenth century, its founder Guru Nanak being followed by nine successors – all called Gurus – whose teachings are embodied in the holy book, *The Guru Granth*. Although there were resemblances to the other two religions in India at the time of Sikhism's founding, the original teachings, in which some Islamic influence can be detected, attacked many of the outward manifestations of Hinduism such as idolatry and ostentatious prayer. Sikhs believe in one God; each makes his or her personal relationship with God and worships in his or her own way, aiming, after many cycles of rebirth, to achieve true understanding and unity with God. As in Islam, Sikhism preaches the equality of all people – irrespective of caste, colour or creed. There are two categories of Sikhs: Saihajdaris and Amritdharis. The former are termed apprentices and are not required to be fully orthodox in their approach; they may or may not keep long hair or wear the other symbols described below. The Amritdharis are those who have been formally baptised and are therefore bound to observe special rules, such as daily attendance at the temple, special prayers, dietary rules and the wearing of the 'five Ks'. These Sikhs are called the Khalsa (Pure ones) and keep the following Ks:

- Kesh – uncut hair;
- Kangha – wooden comb;
- Kara – iron wrist bracelet;
- Kirpan – small sword or dagger;
- Kacha – a special undergarment like shorts or breeches.

As the long hair must be formally tied into a knot at the top of the head, the turban is worn by men and has become inevitably a religious necessity and symbol. There are no hard and fast rules of diet and dress but smoking is strictly forbidden. The Sikh Gurus have laid down general rules on conduct, and food and dress but these are open to personal and sub-group interpretation. Some Sikhs would exclude meat eating but most do eat meat, although not of animals slaughtered by the semitic method (Halal or Kosher). Many Sikhs, like Hindus, do not eat beef and some are fully vegetarian, excluding eggs and fish from their diet.

Sikh festivals

Guru Gobind Singh's Birthday This is the anniversary of the birth of Gobind Singh who was formally enthroned as the tenth Guru at the beginning of the year 1676.

Baisakhi Foundation day* This is the anniversary of the creation of the present form of Sikhism (Khalsa) and the baptism by Guru Gobind Singh of the first five disciples. The ceremony, baptism with sweetened water, is now commonly called Amrit Pan and is an initiation into the Sikh faith.

Diwali: The festival of lights This festival, although a Hindu festival, is of distinct significance to Sikhs, being the anniversary of the release from imprisonment of Guru Hargobind, the sixth Guru, by the Moghal emperor.

Guru Nanak's Birthday This is the anniversary of the birth of the first Guru, the founder of the Sikh religion.

Hinduism

In India, Hinduism is the major religion, followed by some 80 per cent of the population. In Britain, however, Hindus form the smallest of the three main religious groups – about 20 per cent of the Asian population. The majority of Hindus in Britain are Gujeratis coming from India via East Africa.

Hinduism is a complex religion, and its customs and beliefs vary widely both regionally and from class to class. The following notes are therefore a simplification.

For the orthodox Hindu, worship ('Poojah') is centred on the home, and religious and ceremonial rites are performed by the eldest member of the family. Many gods are worshipped but it is believed that, like man, all emanate from one eternal creative force. The religious aim of life is to be drawn back to the divine origin and to be released from the need to be reborn. Reincarnation is, therefore, of central importance, with status in the next life depending on performance in this. This belief underlies the caste system which determines social position and, originally, occupation. Traditionally there are four main caste divisions:

- **Brahmin**, the priestly caste;
- **Kshatriya**, the warrior and ruling class;
- **Vaishya**, the farmers, merchants and craftsmen;
- **Shudra**, the caste of servants.

There are also many sub-castes; each caste is exclusive of the other and intermarriage disapproved of. However, the caste system is breaking down in India and it is now illegal to discriminate on the grounds of caste.

For Hindus, the reading of religious books such as the *Bhagavadgita* and the *Mahabharata* is of significant importance, just as the *Bible* is to Christians and the *Quran* to Muslims. Horoscopes play an integral role in Hinduism; they form part of a pattern of Hindu religious life, involving the choosing of marriage partners and auspicious days for important ceremonies. As in any other religion, not all followers of the Hindu religion observe all the prescribed practices. There are, however, certain social customs and modes of behaviour which need to be understood and respected. Principal among these are personal cleanliness, and methods of cooking and eating. Since the cow is a sacred animal, the eating of beef is strongly forbidden. Most Hindus will not eat fish or eggs, or any foodstuffs made with eggs. Again the drinking of alcohol and the smoking of tobacco are religiously and socially disapproved of.

Hindu festivals

Jaram Ashtami: Birthday of Lord Krishna This is a nativity festival celebrated at midnight with night-long prayers and is held in the temple.

Durga Ashtami This is a night of prayers preceded by a fasting day.

Navratri: Festival of Nine Nights

Dussehra Also referred to as Vijaya – Dashami, this is a widely observed festival followed by Navratri.

Diwali: The festival of lights This festival marks the start of the Hindu new year; a time of giving presents.

Holi: The festival of colours This is observed at the beginning of spring.

Culture and religion – Sikhs, Muslims and Hindus

In terms of religious observance, Muslims, Sikhs and Hindus vary considerably in their attitudes to life. However, with respect to some cultural dimensions, there may be some overlap, and they may be intricately present in the daily repertoire of life. This probably results from the fact that in the Indian sub-continent, and certainly before the partitions of Pakistan and Bangladesh, Indians, Pakistanis and Bengalis lived under the umbrella of a feudal and subsequently imperial Indian state. Thus, one may find similarities among them in matters of dress, and in attitudes to family, marriage and other social customs. To exemplify this point a number of areas have been identified in which all three Asian religious groups share the same social and cultural attitudes. The term Asian will subsequently be used to denote all three groups.

The family

The Asian family in general is an extended family, consisting of mother, father, sons and sons' families. This joint family system usually shares family responsibilities, but all important decisions are always taken by the head of the family unit. In western societies, such a family network is seen as inhibiting individual development; in Asian families, encouraging and nurturing collective development is very important. However, over the past 10 years in Britain, the extended family has been breaking down and the assumption that 'Asians care for their own' is slowly becoming an unreliable tenet.

Marriage

The majority of Asian marriages are arranged. They are regarded as the linking of families rather than of individuals and, therefore, great care is taken by parents to ensure that the families are suited to each other. Equally, great care and much time is spent in finding suitable marriage partners. Parents usually choose partners for their children from families which are known to them, and approved of by them; they then use this knowledge of a family to assess personal and group compatibility.

The system of arranged marriages is often difficult for westerners to understand, coming from a society which endorses the freedom of individuals to choose their marriage partners and where the circles in which young people find their married partners are not chosen by their parents. The arranged marriage, however, takes place within the context of a society which emphasises religious duty and family life despite the negative perception of the west concerning freedom of choice. In addition, it should be noted that many Asian children must give their consent to marriage with the prospective partner before any marriage ceremony can take place.

The marriage ceremony itself is a time of great excitement and great expense. The ceremonies, which are highly symbolic, are crowned by a feast to which as many people as possible are invited. After the ceremony the newly-weds usually go to live with the family of the bridegroom or, if they can afford it, live in their own home in the neighbourhood of his immediate family.

Names

Names and incorrect name calling are a sensitive area for everyone, and if both the names and the naming systems are unfamiliar mistakes can easily occur. Muslims, Sikhs and Hindus have different naming systems. There are also regional differences as well as names which donate caste or sub-caste. Sikh names always include Singh as the middle name for a man and Kaur for a woman. Amongst Hindus, the suffix 'bhai' meaning brother (bhen for sister) is often added to a name amongst close friends, or 'ji' is added as a term of respect. Muslim names frequently include Muhammad, Ahmed, Rashid, for a man, and Fatima and Amina, for a woman; they are mostly religious names which come before or after other surnames. For women Bibi or Begum is usually used at the end of the name to denote female status.

The most familiar Gujerati name is Patel, which occurs with equal frequency as the British surname 'Smith'.

Within the religious naming system, Swami is used for Hindu priests and Imam or Ulmas for Muslim priests.

There are no hard and fast rules about the proper use of Asian names but it is essential that, if in doubt, one should ask.

Language

Asian languages vary considerably both in verbal and written form. On the Indian subcontinent there are about 20 major languages and many more dialects. This means that in many cases Asians from different regions of the same country cannot understand each others' language. In the UK the main Asian languages are Urdu, Gujerati, Punjabi, Hindi, and Bengali (Sylheti), with others including Tamil and Malagalem. It should be noted that many Asians are illiterate and although some Pakistanis and Sikhs speak Punjabi, its written script is completely different from other languages. Though the Kashmiri dialect is similar to Punjabi, it is written in the Urdu/Farsi script.

Unani and Ayurvedic medicine

This is practised in Islamic, Hindu or Sikh traditions and is essentially the traditional medicine of the Indian Subcontinent. The practice of Ayurveda had been considerably modified by the humoural theory of Unani medicine – the four elements, hot-cold, wet-dry – brought by Hakims to the Subcontinent. This practice is also found throughout much of Asia, including China, and has been influenced by Ancient Greek medicine. It is important to acknowledge the long established scientific basis of traditions in alternative medicine which have been in the past, and to the present day remain, integral to the framework of culture and religion. The importance of this on the well-being of its believers has not been understood or valued by western analysts. The role that Hakims and Vaidyas play in Europe in terms of health-related care has yet to be significantly examined in assessing and determining appropriate health services for people from the Indian Subcontinent. However, it is surprising how little attention has been given to the increasing requests for treatment by White middle class people the in UK's Chinatowns and Ayurvedic clinics.

Signpost

The purpose of this chapter has been to demonstrate that the term 'Asian' is often too loosely applied in Britain. Asian people are not all the same; generalisations are inadequate and unacceptable, and individual and group identities need to be given their own status and importance. Although culture is personal, this does not prevent persons from outside an individual culture, who are in the majority and in positions of power, from prejudging and devaluing other systems they feel inferior to their own. In other words there seems to be a dependency on a naturality rather than a social construct which, 'disappears at the moment one recognises one's own customs to be different. Alternatively one privileges oneself, claims a naturality to one's own practices and deems the other persons customs to be wrong, harmful or misguided' (Burghart; 1988).

2. 'He's our child and we shall always love him' – Mental handicap: the parents' response

It is Monday morning and there's a call from a desperate social worker seeking advice on a new referral.

'Hello, how can I help you?'
'Hi, I'm a social worker from x district and I'm wondering if you can help me. Yesterday I received a note from the duty officer about a referral concerning an Asian woman. It seems that she had a forced arranged marriage with a man from Lebanon, and is being evicted from her home – she has three children and is in an extremely distressed state of mind. I would be grateful if you could advise me on the languages she may speak and how I can best empathise with her about her marital situation.'

I asked,

'How do you know she doesn't speak English? And why do you think she's unhappy about her marriage?'
'Well, she's Asian and I thought that all Asian women were forced into marriage at an early age and then expected to have many children. Most of them can't speak English and have difficult relations with their parents – don't they?'

Such a dialogue is not unique and strongly exemplifies how perceptions about Asian people, and Asian women in particular, are formed on the basis of preconceived notions about Asian family life. In this particular case, as a result of misinformation and a dependence on stereotypes, the whole referral had been completely misinterpreted. Here, a simple request – for nursery places for her children, some support from social services while her Pakistani husband was away working in Lebanon, and advice on how she could obtain some council accommodation as her parents' house was a little over-crowded – had created a picture of a poor harassed Asian woman, threatened with eviction from her parents' home and experiencing marital problems with her husband. The fact (as was subsequently discovered) that she was born in Britain and could speak perfect English was given no substance at the time of referral. Equally, the fact that she had been happily married for six years and loved her husband bore no relevance.

Services to Asian people often demonstrate expectations among social workers and health workers which are neither congruent with, nor relevant to, the felt and actual needs of the Asian communities. This is most implicit where expectations are significantly different from one individual to another – especially in the area of mental handicap. Statutory agencies are ideal places either to improve or hinder positive imagery of minority ethnic groups. Of course, many of us have prejudices about something or other and stereotypes do exist, but they become most harmful when they are used as a yardstick to measure and complement irrationality – where social workers are led into errors and into needless problems through tendencies to prejudge people and situations.

The tendency to form judgements about others solely on the basis of racial, ethnic or religious identity lies at the heart of the processes to be examined in this chapter: prejudice/stereotypes and discrimination. First I shall offer definitions for both prejudice and discrimination. As will become apparent, the two are closely related yet are distinct in important ways. Secondly, I shall examine how these two processes are instrumental in inhibiting social workers from providing an appropriate and equal service to Asian clients with a disabled child, and how their understanding of the Asian community and disability is distorted by a lack of understanding about cultural and religious needs – where individuality falls prey to perceived group norms at the expense of the disabled client.

Prejudice/stereotypes and discrimination can also be classified as personal and cultural racism, which are enhanced through institutional racism. Dominelli (1988) uses these three constructs to argue how racism is fed into social work theory and practice. Institutional racism is embedded within an infrastructure, resistant to change as a result of policies and practices installed and perpetuated by White professionals working within the organisation. Institutional racism may be endorsed in any institution, whether it be social work, health, education or in the voluntary sector, through a number of strategies which Dominelli identifies as:

- omission;
- denial;
- decontextualisation;
- dumping;
- the colour-blind approach;
- the patronising approach;
- avoidance.

It is hoped that the information presented in this discussion will be of benefit in two ways: first as a means by which one may understand the nature and causes of both prejudice/stereotypes and discrimination; and secondly, to counteract the negative impact of both on one's own feelings, beliefs and behaviour, not only towards the Asian community but towards the Black community in general.

Prejudice, stereotypes and discrimination – potential bombs?

The terms prejudice and discrimination are often used synonymously in everyday speech. However, prejudice generally refers to negative attitudes of a special kind; in contrast, discrimination describes negative actions directed against the persons who are its objects – the victims of prejudice.

Prejudice is an attitude (wholly negative) towards the members of some specific group (racial, ethnic, religious and so on) that causes the persons holding it to assume other negatives solely on the basis of membership of that group. Since attitudes often operate as frameworks for organising or recalling information, persons who are prejudiced tend to notice and only remember certain kinds of information about the groups they dislike – 'facts that are largely negative in nature'. When prejudice is defined it refers to the beliefs and expectations an individual holds about the members of a particular group. Often these beliefs and expectations form clusters of preconceived notions known as stereotypes. Unfortunately, once they are formed, stereotypes lead individuals to assume that all members of a racial, ethnic, religious or other group, possess similar traits or act in the same manner. In short, stereotypes lead persons who hold them to ignore important differences between unique individuals. This can involve tendencies to act in negative ways towards the persons who are the objects of such attitudes and these, translated into overt actions, constitute discrimination.

Discrimination often takes open and direct forms, however, it is also frequently much more subtle in nature. That is, even highly prejudiced individuals seek to conceal their negative feelings, expressing them openly only in situations where they think they can safely 'get away' with harmful actions towards disliked groups. While many forms of subtle discrimination exist, two are deserving of specific attention in the context of this study:

- the withholding of aid from people who need it; and
- the performance of trivial or tokenistic actions.

Both of these are extremely important in determining and predicting the provision of services to Asian families who have a disabled child. For example, many social workers assume that Asian families do not require respite care services since this is already structured within the extended family system; thus, they may withhold aid from people who need it. Tokenism also occurs, that is the effort involved to promote better services is minimal, but enough to constitute a means of continued discrimination: 'Haven't I done enough for those people already – after all I use an interpreter on my visits'.

Throughout our lives we rely on our values, beliefs and norms of behaviour to assist us in analysing and preparing what we hope will be an adequate response to persons who are, in some way, perceived to be different from us. In terms of delivering a service this may result in a worker drawing upon a pool of stereotypes in order to administer help in an 'acceptable' way. As discussed earlier, this can create problems for both the provider and the user. During the course of this research it was found that stereotypes played an important role in confusing social workers about the needs of Asian parents, and more importantly about the attitude of these parents towards their handicapped children.

'Look behind the word Asian and see me'

Social workers have various expectations of how Asian parents view their mentally/physically handicapped child. In recent years efforts have been directed towards what many believe to be the single most significant barrier – that of attitudes. If attitudes can be changed, solutions to the specific problems confronting disabled children and their parents will fall into place as a matter of course. Associated with attitudes, the general level of knowledge among social workers is of decisive importance to the quantity and quality of the services they offer. Where ignorance and adherence to inappropriate beliefs prevail, there is low motivation to develop services and even sometimes a hostile attitude towards the Asian community in general. However, there are some practitioners in the caring services, who work to a model of practice by challenging stereotypes, through consultation with members or workers from the community in which they are involved and by their own personal commitment.

By looking at various verbatim comments from social workers, a range of attitudes about Asian parents and disability can be demonstrated. It is important to note here that such attitudes clearly indicate the anxiety and frustration of dealing with a client group where the only information one can draw upon is based on stereotypes, assumptions and hearsay. In brief these stereotypes include assumptions such as:

- Asian parents reject their child immediately on finding out that he or she has a disability or disabilities;
- Asian parents encounter feelings of resentment from other members of their family;
- Asian parents feel stigmatised by the community;
- Asian parents see the birth of a disabled child as a punishment for sins or a test from God;
- Asian parents suffer feelings of inadequacy, especially the mother;
- Asian parents express embarrassment;
- Asian parents fail to see a necessity to prepare for the future welfare of the child, that is they feel God will protect him or her;
- the Asian male is the dominant figure of the household and all communications should be made through him;
- parents show little interest in using toys to develop the child's abilities;
- parents depend on the extended family to provide care to disabled children;
- Asian parents don't understand the necessity for genetic counselling – there are too many inter-family marriages.

Although there are some Asian parents who express and confirm the above stereotypes, these attitudes are not absolute or representative of all Asian parents. Such stereotypical attitudes are also frequently reported by White parents with children with disabilities. Therefore, for any service provider it is essential that individual needs are given priority and the importance of parents' views be acknowledged.

Let us now move away from paraphrasing stereotypes to accurate information and actual quotes. These were taken from various social workers in response to the question, 'What difficulties do you encounter when working with Asian parents?' The following includes details of further common assumptions held by the social workers questioned:

- **Language** 'Some parents do not speak English or their English is limited. Mothers seem less likely to speak English. As the mother is sometimes a key figure it is not possible to discuss problems directly with her. Children can be used to interpret. Fathers/ husbands also do this but the accuracy of their information about, or knowledge of problems may be questionable.'
- **Ideas** 'The acceptance of services (for example, respite care) may not be appropriate to the family and culture of Asian people. Their attitudes to the needs of handicapped children may differ from ours because of cultural views about handicap. Containing problems within the family is preferred to asking for help.'
- 'Working with Asian families presents two major difficulties, **communication** being one. I have no knowledge of Urdu/Punjabi and quite often only one or two family members will speak limited English (usually male). In these circumstances it is difficult to discuss either the situation in depth or the feelings of other family members.'
- '**Cultural differences** cause the second major difficulty. I have only sparse knowledge of the Eastern cultures and, therefore, of the general attitude of families faced with the difficulties presented by a handicapped member. Acceptance/repetition, involvement of outside agencies, sharing of care: is it likely that such families would welcome involvement with non-Asiatic families because of the particular cultural/religious difficulties?'
- '**Asian parents** of disabled children usually do not have a positive or encouraging attitude; rather it is mostly one of shame or fear of social scorn and stigmatisation, coupled with an almost religious or superstitious view of disability as a manifestation of the will of God – and even in some instances, of the wrath of God for their own prior sins.'

- 'In working with Asian families a great problem is language, particularly with Asian females, which exacerbates the difficulties of sensitivity to the attitudes and values that operate within the family.'
- 'Empathic dissonance thus creates problems of deployment of resources in the most appropriate and effective way, particularly when dealing with behavioural aspects and attempting to devise modifying programmes to reduce or eliminate anti-social behaviour. (There are also myths which tend to be attached to Asian families in general and which set up prior expectations in people's minds.'
- 'Given that communication is important and that this is often difficult, the barriers to understanding are considerable; cultural differences complicate this and create further barriers.'
- 'Occasionally finding difficulty in speaking to both parents together – in my experience the mother and female members of the family are prominent in relation to children, and fathers were absent.'
- 'Negative attitudes are held towards outside support as opposed to community or family support.'

For Asian parents such comments are common and easily recognised as part of an assumptions/panic syndrome – though they are not as easily understood. I use this terminology to demonstrate what happens when one is faced with a client whose culture is unfamiliar, whose needs are assumed based on stereotypes and this causes panic when these assumed needs are proved wrong. Of course the extent to which such feelings expressed by social workers hold true depends very much on the amount of contact and the degree of experience the social worker has had. From the initial point of view of the research undertaken in this area, many of these attitudes have been challenged, and redirected to other sources to explain their frequency and confirmation.

Disability, whether it is physical, mental, sensory or auditory, is not prejudiced in any way: it transcends all races, beliefs and cultures. It creates similarly profound emotional, practical and psychological experiences for all parents, whoever they are. Unfortunately, where Asian families are concerned, common sense about a valid generalisation of attitudes towards disability is lost in the mists of ignorance and perceived cultural differences. Little or no attention is given to what is in fact a natural and universal response to having a child who is born with a disability or who, later on in childhood, is diagnosed as 'disabled'. Looking for differences where none exist or assuming homogeneity of feelings when differences need to be identified is a form of cultural racism.

Throughout this research, and as exemplified by many of the anecdotes, communication has been highlighted as the main barrier in preventing adequate assessments and the building up of relationships between social worker and parents. While for a few of the parents interviewed in this study language did pose some problems, the majority of parents had a good command of English and for some, English was their first language. In spite of this, communication problems persisted; cross-purposes increased and a general situation of misunderstanding between parent and social worker was encountered. However, the problem is often not generated by the parent: it derives frequently from the inability of the social worker to recognise meanings because of strong accents and bias. Where interpreters are used, social workers may be reluctant to depend on the accuracy of the information translated. It has often been said by professional interpreters that they are not used often enough by social workers and other professionals in cases where English is poor. This in itself may convey how personal racism often prevents the intervention of bi-lingual workers to assist in assessing Asian families' needs. There are a number of issues and problems surrounding interpreters and these are discussed in more detail in Chapter 5.

Evidence also suggests that the assumption of Asian male dominance is not irrefutable. Many Asian women who were interviewed indicated that their husbands were the sole communicators with social agencies but that this did not imply that they were unaware of what had been discussed. All decisions were shared decisions, and both parents shared the caring and responsibility for their child. Where fathers were absent during some social workers visits, this was usually a consequence of employment rather than a lack of interest or responsibility. It is important to remember here that where mothers are seen to be playing a quiet and passive role, it does not mean that they are illustrations of the stereotype of the subservient Asian woman. The mother is concerned about her child, shows an increased interest to communicate, but may decide not to for fear of being ridiculed because her standard of English is poor. In response to views concerning the extended family network and the assumed preference to refuse outside help, these are again the product of myth. Such a caricature is founded on a vision of the White British family, which stresses that it is open and non-patriarchal. It is clear that Asian parents do not utilise services to their fullest potential, but this is not necessarily because they have their own resources; rather, they may not want to be accused of being a burden on the state and taking more than their share. Similarly, they may be reluctant to sit down and explain the importance of their religious and cultural identity to social workers.

Counselling for Asian parents is also fraught with difficulties as they may be subject to victimisation and cultural racism such as statements that 'first cousin marriages are always prone to producing a child with some disability, so why do these people do it?' The genetic risks of marriages between family members are frequently raised with regard to the Asian community. Inter-family marriages do not necessarily lead to an increased risk of inherited disease or disability. However, Asian families – like those from other racial backgrounds – **may** be at risk if there is already a family history of congenital disability or an inherited disease. In the past few years there has been general concern that **all** parents of whatever racial or cultural background should have access to information on the possible risks of genetically determined diseases. The option of genetic counselling should be available for those who wish it and should be provided sensitively by someone familiar with the views and values of the families concerned. The possibility of gene therapy being introduced within the next few years (which may make some disabilities and diseases treatable before birth) is likely to raise the public debate about how parents are told of possible risks and what advice they are given about further action. Open and honest discussion with people who are known to work in the community will be essential to avoid misconceptions and to ensure that any advice is relevant, non-judgemental and fully accurate.

Similarly, behavioural programmes for young children are based on White cultural behavioural patterns; there is no scope for integrating other cultures and this results in providing inappropriate skills for children from an Asian background. For example, teaching a child with a mental handicap to eat with a knife, fork and spoon can sometimes leave him and his parents completely at a loss, since most

Asian children who eat Asian food do so with their hands and not with cutlery.

Social workers and psychologists might assume that the absence of toys in the living room suggests that toys are not seen as important by parents, in assisting the development of their child's motor or sensory skills. It may be that the toys are kept upstairs or in another room, so it is always better to ask rather than to assume the worst. The social skill development and cognitive development of their disabled children are as important to Asian parents as to other parents; like all parents they realise the need to address the future welfare of their child, but they may find services to enable this to be estranged from their cooperation and understanding. Religious belief here is very strong: that God will provide for him/her is not questioned. However, at the same time, they realise that responsibility for the future of their child must be undertaken by them and they should therefore take the initiative in preparation for him or her – with or without the help of a social worker.

At this point, a number of social workers I interviewed have commented on how disabled Asians are prepared for marriage. In some cases, the girls have severe mental handicaps and are totally dependent on their carers and this may be considered on two levels. First, securing a marriage partner for their daughter will serve to relax and provide some comfort to parents who will be reassured that, after their death, someone will be looking after their daughter; secondly, it suggests that some parents are not fully aware of the degree of disability their daughter has and that the condition is incurable and will never be normal. The latter is probably due to poor parent counselling at the identification of disability, and ineffective health and social work intervention to educate parents about the prognosis for their child.

Lack of social contact between White and Asian parents has also been highlighted as a point of concern. Attitudes among Asian parents with a disabled child are probably no different from those of their White counterparts. Most of the big voluntary agencies which are said to assist parents who have a child with a disability display an under-representation of Asian people; these agencies find it difficult to develop appropriate strategies to welcome Asian families as members.

On the basis of such attitudes as those discussed, it is not surprising that Asian parents feel judged even before they have had their first visit from social workers or other practitioners in the health and social work settings. For this reason many Asian parents have a particular difficulty in seeking the assistance of social services because they feel that their cultural beliefs or religious needs will be ignored, misunderstood or ridiculed. Rather than face this type of situation, they prefer to withdraw from using statutory services. The emphasis is on individuality; they don't wish to be placed in the 'pool of generalisations'. And they would rather not be told that 'Mrs Dutt didn't wish her child to be taken into short-term care' – for them, Mrs Dutt does not speak for the whole Asian community.

Asian parents no longer accept the reasoning used to deprive them of their uniqueness – stereotypes which may categorise Asians and provide some social workers with an overall impression about Asians and their expectations regarding behaviour, may be used to render their social work task easier; but Asian parents will no longer allow it to justify their actions or to perpetuate further discriminatory practices against them. So 'Look behind the word *Asian* and see *me*'.

Signpost

The role that stereotypes play obviously changes according to the cycle of conscious and unconscious realism applied to them. This is subject to the transient nature of racist attitudes and what determines acceptable or inappropriate patterns of behaviour. Throughout this chapter, stereotypes have been demonstrated in various forms. To the reader some may have appeared too extreme and unrepresenta- tive, and therefore inapplicable. However, the purpose of using these stereotypes was to indicate, first, the reaction of many of the interviewed, social workers in their assessment of the Asian com- munity; and secondly, and more importantly, they were used to indicate the strength and propensity of piecemeal information, incorrectly fed into social work strategies.

To conclude this chapter a fictional case study will be described. Many of the points discussed in this chapter will be highlighted and, to avoid repetition, this section will close on a series of questions for the reader to consider.

Case study

Mrs Hardy had completed her training as a health visitor and her first visit was to Mrs Choudhry, who is a Bengali Hindu mother of two daughters. The elder daughter was born with cerebral palsy and there is concern that the second daughter is showing signs of hearing impairment. While visiting the home at 9.00 a.m. Mrs Hardy noticed that the mother appeared to be inattentive towards the children, that they were poorly dressed and their faces dirty, and she remembered that their younger child, aged two, had not attended the clinic for her second hearing test. Mrs Choudhry speaks very little English and when the health visitor enquired about her missing the appointment, the mother showed her a number of unopened brown envelopes. Due to the difficulties with language, the health visitor left the home with a prospective strategy for action. Her first resolution was to arrange an ESL tutor as she felt the mother would benefit from this and some genetic counselling. She also thought that the social worker involved with the family should know that the mother was showing signs of post-natal depression, probably prompted by family pressures on the mother to have a boy.

The social worker, Mr Kavanagh, called to see Mrs Choudhry to inform her that her elder daughter had been allocated a place at Springfields Special School. However, no-one opened the door, even though Mr Kavanagh could see Mrs Choudhry behind the curtain in the front window. He put a note through the door to say that he had called, asking Mrs Choudhry to contact him.

A fortnight elapsed and Mr Kavanagh decided to visit the home again but this time with his team's receptionist Miss Khan, who is a young Asian woman. This time they gained access at 7.00 p.m., but there was still a communication problem as Miss Khan is an Urdu speaker. Fortunately, Mrs Choudhry understands a little of this language and was able to respond to some of the questions being asked. On this occasion the social worker noted the dampness in the one-bedroomed flat and the pile of dirty washing and dishes lying next to the broken immersion heater.

Mrs Choudhry is obviously distressed and needs support. The children are under constant care; either they are being carried by the mother as she tries to do general housework or they are lying over her when she sits down.

Questions
- What stereotypes are being used?
  - by the health visitor;
  - by the social worker.

- Did the workers respond to the language problem appropriately? List their responses as good or bad practice. What would you have done?
- Describe your impression of Mr Choudhry and his relationship to the family.
- What indications are there of the socio-economic status of Mrs Choudhry? What services could be allocated to the family which were absent?
- Using the above case study, how would you assess the problems encountered by the mother had she been White?
- Show how race and culture have been centralised, without taking into account other peripheral factors, which are equally important in indicating these types of scenarios.

3. 'Social workers never listen' – Social workers: how parents perceive them

The carer of a child with a disability must undergo much strain, anxiety and self-discipline in order to acquire the coping skills needed to assist them with this great task. However, when the carer is Asian these stresses are greatly increased as he or she is also faced with institutional, personal, and cultural racism, and the perceived stigma both their own culture and the indigenous culture attach to disability. Communication difficulties often mean that Asian parents are not fully aware or informed about the causation, diagnosis and prognosis of their child's handicap. Therefore it is not surprising that this leads parents to assume that their child will be cured even if, for example, their child has Downs Syndrome.

When discussing the needs of an Asian child with a disability, the bureaucratic approach is prominent; differences in attitude are considered as cultural and problematical – but still the services are said to be equally distributed and available, even though the reality falls far short of this goal.

Services are sometimes alienated from the cultural and religious needs of a population they are supposed to be serving. Within the Asian community there is consensus of thought which describes the present state of affairs as follows: 'Social workers and other workers in the caring professions are there to provide a service; whether that service caters for the religious and cultural needs of the Asian community is not their concern – they can only offer what exists within the current service package. While they realise the frustration this must cause, they can only sympathise and do nothing more'. Some local authorities have tried to create a positive image of themselves by saying that they are addressing the problems at hand and shall hopefully be implementing an equal opportunities policy to ensure equality, appropriateness and acceptability of service provision. For Asian parents with a disabled child such gestures, incomplete in themselves, are seen as commonplace and have been responsible for an apparent lack of trust and confidence in the social services.

Results from this research are mixed: while some parents directed and attached blame to the individual social worker, there was a general understanding that the source of the problem lay within the organisational network of social services themselves – administration and management were seen to be equally responsible, if not more so. Attitudes towards social workers ranged from positive assessments of them as helpful, understanding, good-willed and empathic to resentment and accusations of lack of sensitivity, bias, racism and lack of caring. At first parents did show some reluctance to convey their true feelings about social workers and so confidentiality about what they were saying had to be re-confirmed. Many of the comments illustrated the points made above and were very emotional in content and projection. An extract from one of the interviews exemplifies this point.

Case study

The case concerns a Hindu family and their five-year-old daughter; the words were recorded as the father and mother spoke them and indicate quite strongly the lack of information about their daughter's disabilities and the desperation of the parents in their efforts to help her.

Medical history

'She was born under weight so her development is delayed physically, she has speech problems, she can't speak properly; she is under hospital in special care.

Description of condition

'She is not mentally handicap but she is handicap – not physically strong, she can't walk properly, she got tired very soon, she is under in hospital in special care. She put the special shoes on she got it from the hospital; every three months her feet checked up.

General information

> 'She has chest infection since birth, during winter she always sick; our house got damp, so she always sick. Nobody listen to our problem we apply for a council [house] but nobody listen to our problem.'

From this dialogue three important issues arise; some have been referred to earlier but, in order to get the message across, need to be repeated. First, the strong emotional feeling the parents have for their child's welfare is apparent. Secondly, they lack information about the etiology of the disabilities and what this means for the child's future. This is clearly indicated by the repetition used to describe their daughter's disability. Finally, there is a sense of the utter helplessness the parents experience because they can find no substantial support services – there is no one they can turn to who will give them a positive response.

This case is not an isolated one and other parents echoed the same concerns; for them social workers seemed ineffective people who were unsympathetic and ignorant of the plight of Asian parents. Poor housing conditions, unequal health care, and high unemployment are areas which are not considered in assessments of families, many of whom have had to survive on the minimum of benefits and services for their disabled children. The amount and frequency of contact Asian parents had with their child's social worker reinforced many of the well-established negative attitudes parents had towards them. Though most parents had a social worker, for many, visits were rare and the information they gave about services was limited. Again to demonstrate this let us return to the Hindu family in the case study.

Case study continued

> 'Do you have a social worker?'
> 'Yes, but she never visits to our house or listen to our problem.'
> 'Do you have problems explaining what you want to a social worker? Why?'
> 'We had many problems. She don't want to know about anything.'
> 'Do you feel social workers care about your problems?'
> 'No, she never listens to our problems.'
> 'If you have a social worker, how often do you see him/her?'
> 'Once in a year, she do not come.'
> 'Would you like to have a social worker?'
> 'Yes, please.'

Expectations about what social workers can offer are very low. Undoubtedly *support* is the key word and is not measured in monetary terms. Regular contact with a social worker who understands their problems, and is in a position to offer services which are sensitive to cultural and religious diversities, is all that is asked.

In the preceding chapters I have addressed the problems created by racism and stereotypes. In this section I shall look at two examples of social work intervention: one which is largely negative in context, and another which is very positive and offers an excellent example of good social work practice. Throughout this chapter I shall be giving my own interpretations of the attitudes expressed by Asian parents concerning social workers on the basis of their responses to my questionnaire, so at this point it may be helpful to refer to the summation of these results and the original questionnaire reproduced in Appendices 1 and 2.

What about those parents who receive nothing from statutory or voluntary agencies because they are unaware of their entitlement to them? This question has a direct bearing on a case encountered during my research:

Case study

One family, who had recently moved into Birmingham from Halifax, had a twelve-year-old son who was mentally handicapped, partially-sighted and suffered from a hearing impairment. Both parents spoke no English and relied on neighbours for help. The father worked in a factory and so, though money was coming in to the home, income was low. Total care for their son was undertaken by the parents and some members of the Asian community, with no assistance from social services or the health service. It was not until another parent I was interviewing asked me whether I had visited this family that they became known to the social services. Surprised that their names had not been included on my list, I took this up with the social services department. They, however, had not heard of this family and became very concerned. The same day, arrangements were made to visit the family and assess their needs.

This type of situation all too readily demonstrates the necessity to promote an awareness among the Asian community about the range of services offered for disabled children and adults.

Education and training also has an instrumental role to play, not just for the parents, but for the service providers as well. The providers of services need to be prepared to create a service delivery system which will attract rather than hinder Asian parents from its use. Terminology is extremely important here as this can jeopardise and distort the real meaning attached to some services. For example, for those parents lucky enough to be offered short-term care for their disabled children, the word 'care' may be misinterpreted as something which is legally binding rather than voluntary. Hence parents may feel extremely reluctant to use this service, believing it to be threatening to the future home care of their child.

Equally a great deal of credibility is lost when social workers fail to provide detailed information about special provisions made for children who have dietary needs. One parent told me that she was informed by her social worker that her son had been given a place in a registered care home for the weekend. Although preparation had been made by the mother to arrange for Halal food for her son, it was not until she reached the home that she was told by the officer in charge that there was no need as all dietary requirements were arranged for.

Social workers, I have found, agree that they sometimes miss out vital details which would effectively resolve many of the problems that they encounter when dealing with Asian families. It would also be far easier for parents to accept service intervention if they were assured that their child's religious and cultural needs were being catered for.

Although communication problems do arise, social workers tend to be perceived as unconcerned about achieving any great depth of understanding in interviewing Asian families, even when interpreters are used. The communication is still limited as the development of rapport between parent and social worker becomes problematic. Parents feel that social workers should make more efforts to break down the barriers of language, colour and cultural difference. Once this is done the needs will become clear and practical help will emerge. An excellent example of this approach in action, resulting in effective social work practice, is discussed in the following case study.

Case study

This is the case of a Pakistani family where one of the three children, all under five, had Downs Syndrome. The family lived in an apartment rented to them by a friend. The father worked in a factory on a part-time basis because he suffered from ill-health. Economically the family was living 'below the breadline'; they were a proud family and did not like to accept charity – even when that 'charity' was actually an entitlement.

A social worker visited the family to assess the family needs, and to check that the three-year-old boy who had Downs Syndrome was receiving adequate care.

For this social worker these people were her first Asian clients, and she knew that there was a lot of information about the religious and cultural needs of the family that she needed to understand. When she first knocked on their front door she assumed that they would know who she was and why she was visiting, as she had sent a letter to the parents informing them of her visit. However, what she did not know was that neither parent could read English and, therefore, they were not aware of her visit. Nevertheless, the social worker was invited into the home by the mother, who spoke very little English.

After satisfying herself that the children were all well, the social worker made a conscious decision to assist this family in the best way she could. First, she arranged for an interpreter to visit the parents with her. From this meeting an accurate assessment of the family's entitlement to various social security benefits was made and this was later explained fully to both parents. The interpreter was also very helpful in explaining the role of the social worker and the various services available for their child from social services, the health authority and voluntary agencies.

In this particular case the social worker wished to develop the relationship further by visiting the family on her own without the aid of an interpreter. This was because she wanted to understand the cultural and religious background of the family to ensure that she was being sensitive – she was trying her best to bridge the cultural gap. In order to do this, she told me that she had often told the mother how she enjoyed Asian food and how she would very much appreciate it if she would give her Asian cookery lessons. It was then decided that in return for being taught to cook Asian food, the social worker would teach the mother English. The first lesson was how to cook chicken, and the social worker had promised to go and buy it. However, when the mother saw it she said, 'No, no can't eat'. At first the social worker was baffled until she realised that Muslims only eat Halal meat, that is meat from animals which are killed in a special religious way.

From this case study one can see how easy it is to develop an understanding of each other, simply by persevering and using resources either in one's profession or in the community. The social worker acknowledged her own lack of information, and she reduced this lack by taking on the responsibility of finding out as much as she could about her clients' background, cultural and social welfare needs. Relationships between Asian parents and social workers are important and, indeed, for some they are extremely good; but for others the relationship can be a poor or negative one. In terms of providing support for parents, the relationship is of vital importance.

Respite care is an essential service to promote to those families who have more than one disabled member who requires continuous care and supervision. Often, information about services of this kind and the type of comfort they offer to parents is shared with other Asian parents who have a disabled child. In this way, by word of mouth recommendation, trust is built up and it becomes a reliable means for other parents to feel secure in using the same service. However, differences may occur in that parents may agree to receive respite care for boys but not for girls. This is mostly due to parents' concerns about the carers of their daughters while they are in short-term homes. Assurances that their daughters will be cared for by female carers is needed, especially for undressing and washing.

In order to identify this concern, I arranged to meet one of the officers in charge of a short-stay home for mentally handicapped children. I asked whether it would be possible to arrange for female carers to wash and undress female residents. In response I was told that it depended on the number of staff available and the degree of sexual awareness of the resident in question. This leads to questions of how do you measure sexual awareness in a mentally handicapped child? And who has the right to make decisions about a mentally handicapped person's sexuality, simply because they cannot do so for themselves? One parent had feared that her daughter with severe learning difficulties could have been abused by a male staff member in her residential respite care home. Some Asian families may feel strongly that male carers should not be responsible for the personal care of girls and women and could be unhappy using services where mixed care is usual practice. When their child is in respite care, parents usually assume that the child becomes the responsibility of the local authority, and that staff would ensure his/her safety as well as observing their cultural and religious requirements. But unless the local authority can provide carers for female residents, the fear of this happening to an Asian daughter will remain.

In this same context, similar concerns and reservations apply to the fostering of mentally handicapped children in short-term care. Asian parents feel they are not given equal rights to say where their children can or cannot be placed. Many argue that if they ask for their son or daughter to be placed in an Asian foster home where the prospective parents share the language, culture and religion of the child, these requests are not met by social workers. Social workers argue that this cannot be done because there are not enough Asian foster parents registered with them, or because their stay is only short and the aim is to offer 'space' to parents rather than long-term involvement of others in the care of their children. Like many of the explanations put forward to explain what is, in effect, a form of discrimination for children in care, some workers fail to recognise the undue haste and insensitivity demonstrated in placing Asian children in foster homes.

The picture is not a completely bleak one: there are social workers who understand the problems Asians are facing, and have attempted to alleviate some of them by learning to speak Urdu in their spare time or demanding training in skills which will equip them to provide adequate and appropriate support and counselling. Local authorities vary but some still need to break away from a perception of themselves as tolerant do-gooders improving the quality of life for Asian families, by challenging their own racism and assumption-making tactics. Some social workers themselves are beginning to redress the balance and are challenging their managers to do more in this respect. The Asian community will no longer resign itself to passively accept poor quality services; nor will they allow social workers and others to continue the process of pre-judgement of their needs.

Certainly the scale of the problem demands more imagination and effort on the part of the DSS. Investments in community-based services which are sensitive to the needs of the people for whom they

are intended should be given a higher profile and policy commitment. Unless and until a positive move is made in this direction,
social workers will continue to be perceived by the Asian community
as insensitive to their needs.

Signpost

In this study the attitudes of parents to social workers have been
based on their own contact with them, and their feelings about the
type of services they can provide. A recurring theme throughout this
work has been social workers' own acknowledgement that services
are eurocentric in nature and, therefore, inappropriate to Asian
families. However, in spite of this Asian parents still want to know
what their child is entitled to, and they should then be given the
opportunity to say yes or no to these entitlements. To demonstrate
this further and to enhance some of the points already made in this
chapter, a number of cases will be looked at under headings of
Respite care; Diagnosis/terminology; Benefits; and Social workers.

Respite care (including day care and short-term fostering)

• Rafique's parents do not like the idea of giving their child to
  someone else because they feel that they should care for him
  without anyone's help. However, because their son has severe
  behavioural problems in addition to his mental and physical
  handicap, he is difficult to control and his parents need a break.
  Initially the father was very reluctant to send his son to respite care
  because he thought his dietary needs would not be met. Social
  workers arranged for Halal food and now Rafique attends a day
  centre once a week. Sometimes he stays over the weekend and
  facilities are arranged accordingly.

• Sheilah is a Downs Syndrome child and her parents do not allow
  her to have respite care – they feel happier when the child is with
  them as they know what her needs are. Relatives of the family help
  with Sheilah when asked to and do so regularly. During school
  holidays Sheilah is sent to a day centre to encourage her
  development and social skills.

• Feroza is now 18 years of age. Her parents have never been
  informed about respite care and have said it is not needed because
  they obtain support from family members.

- Anil, who is 12-years-old and suffers from severe learning difficulties and is physically disabled, has never had respite care. He lives in an extended family, and his parents have to provide much support and help for Anil with toileting, carrying him up and down stairs, and playing with him so he doesn't feel depressed. They have not been informed about either respite care or day care.

- Mrs Haji had not heard of respite care, although once it had been explained, she said that her social worker had arranged fostering for her son, Abdul. The parents were introduced to many families who offered to foster Abdul for short periods. Mr and Mrs Haji were able to meet with them several times before they allowed their son to be fostered. The foster parents were very good with Abdul and they all got on very well with each other. Unfortunately, this family has moved and Abdul was allocated to another family; however, there were no children in the second foster family and Abdul got bored, so fostering was stopped. Mr and Mrs Haji think fostering is a good idea because it gives them a chance to have some free time and to give attention to their other two children. Ideally they would like an Asian foster family which has the same cultural and religious background as theirs and can speak their home language.

- Amara is 11-years-old and is mentally and physically disabled. Her parents do not agree with respite care because their daughter would have to mix with members of the opposite sex. They used to have a female carer who visited the home once a week, and helped with bathing and exercising Amara. The parents would like to have a carer because Amara is putting on weight and is becoming too big to be carried. There are four other children in the family and they are all boys; Amara's parents do not feel it is correct for them to see their sister naked and preparing for a bath.

Diagnosis/terminology
- Mrs Chaudhry's son has Downs Syndrome. When the doctors made their diagnosis she did not understand why they kept on repeating that he would have learning difficulties and other health

related problems. Mrs Chaudhry knew that her son looked 'Chinese' but did not feel that this should label him as disabled in any way. At the time she was experiencing this anxiety and confusion there was no interpreter or bi-lingual counsellor who would help her.

- Haroon was born with muscular atrophy, but his parents were not fully informed about his diagnosis and it wasn't until two years later that they began to understand exactly what this disability meant. There was no counselling, and neither their health visitor nor their social worker were felt to be sympathetic and sensitive to the parents' needs.

- Mrs Patel cannot read, write or speak English and when her daughter was born mentally handicapped her husband was away in India. There were no interpreters available at the time of diagnosis and although the doctor explained what the abnormality was, she did not understand. When her husband returned a few weeks after the birth he contacted his GP and was then told exactly what the diagnosis was for their daughter. When Mrs Patel was told she said that the GP was telling lies and deliberately making them upset: 'My daughter was born normal and now they are saying something is wrong. If that is the case the doctors must have given her some medicine which has made her disabled'.

Benefits
- Mrs Khan receives Income Support, Mobility Allowance and Attendance Allowance for Safida who is severely mentally hand-icapped. Mrs Khan is also entitled to Invalid Care Allowance but had not been informed about it; in fact she only applied for the other benefits when she overheard a conversation between two mothers on one of her visits to the hospital.

- Balkee's parents do receive benefits but they do not know exactly why they are entitled to them. At first they did not wish to apply for any because they felt that it was charity but their friends told them that they needed the financial help. Neither parent could

read or write English and it was friends in the community who
assisted them in filling in the relevant forms.

- Mr and Mrs Ahmed did not apply for benefits for two-and-a-half
  years because they were convinced their son was normal. It was
  their social worker who eventually helped them, but they could
  not get any of their benefits backdated.

Social workers

- The last time Mr and Mrs Shabbaz saw their social worker was
  two years ago. They would like to have one because they want to
  be informed about services and they need reassurance that they
  are caring for their children appropriately.

- Mr and Mrs Haji agree that in most cases social workers have
  informed them of the benefits to which they are entitled.
  However, they feel that there is no clear plan to their approach and
  do not make routine visits. They seem to them to be unsympathetic and lacking any interest in understanding the family or their
  cultural and religious needs.

- Mr and Mrs Zamen have never seen their social worker but they
  rely on their community nurse who is Asian. She is seen to be very
  helpful and keeps them up-to-date on services and benefits. She
  fills in forms for them and acts as an interpreter with the DSS.

- Mr Ahmed argues that social workers are unsupportive. The
  family once had a very good social worker who understood their
  problems but she was promoted and never replaced. If the family
  has problems they try to rectify them alone and will only
  contacting social services as a last resort.

- Mrs Bibi doesn't know how she would have coped if it wasn't for
  her social worker. She is Asian, very understanding and an
  effective counsellor. Whenever Mrs Bibi needs help or clarification on services or benefits she contacts her social worker. Every
  night Mrs Bibi prays for her old social worker who is White; he
  knew that she would be better off with someone who could
  communicate with her in her own language and therefore referred

her case to his Asian colleague. Mrs Bibi still sees him occasionally and always thanks him.

- Haroon, who is partially deaf and physically handicapped, looks forward to visits from his social worker. Although he is not Asian he is very caring and smiles a lot. Whenever he can, he brings an interpreter with him and sends Haroon's parents information about benefits and services in their language.

4. 'Information for whom?' – Knowledge of services available from the local authority

The acquisition of knowledge gives the strength, confidence and the ability to communicate needs. It also gives the opportunity to enquire and, more importantly, to ask for information on particular concerns. In some situations the possession of knowledge is assumed to be the same for everyone; this is especially true in the context of service provision for Asian parents of a child with special needs. A wealth of information exists in this area but its dissemination and appropriateness to clients and parents whose first language is not English, is often insignificant, ineffective and drastically limited. Most information whether written or spoken is based on a White literate frame of reference. This inevitably excludes some potential clients from minority ethnic groups. It is not surprising, therefore, that certain services and benefits are not taken up or enquired about – or in some cases, simply not given by the 'provider' because they are considered to be culturally inappropriate.

Before addressing this issue in more detail, it would be useful to examine the services which should be available to clients and their families where severe learning difficulties (SLD) are apparent. This can then be used to demonstrate the problems of Asian parents, both, in obtaining information about services and in assessing its importance and relevance to their individual needs.

Social service provision for clients with a severe learning difficulty (SLD)

Local authority social service departments are only one of a range of statutory and voluntary agencies which can provide services to people with severe learning difficulties; health authorities and some voluntary organisations are particularly active. For example, some social services have increased their facilities in day care services whereas health authorities have responded by appointing more community nurses, psychologists, occupational therapists and so on to work with people with SLD. These professionals may work from a separate base and initially may have created their own contacts in the community with this client group.

As a result of the current Government's financial constraints on local authorities, concern has been expressed that there has been little scope to undertake new approaches to caring for people with SLD and who remain in the care of their parents or who are looking for alternative accommodation in the community. In some areas local authorities have contracted out the provision of services – residential and community – to voluntary organisations such as Barnardo's. In others, community mental handicap teams have been established through joint ventures between the local authority and the health authority; here responsibility would be taken for a whole range of services. Thus services in any local authority area are probably made up of a combination of provisions by the local authority, the health authority, the education authority and the voluntary sector. The balance and interlinking between these in terms of size, services and individual contributions will be influenced by a number of factors such as service history, the level of resources available and the level of professional commitment.

As to the level or quality of provision by individual local authorities, this may be influenced not only by limitations on spending but also as a result of organisational patterns. If the social services department organises its fieldwork services by means of generic, patch-based teams then it will probably offer less provision and less 'expertise' in certain neighbourhoods than a department that has specialist teams or a community mental handicap team. Re-organisation into specialist teams often brings about a 'better' service because teams have a clearer focus of work with people with SLD; furthermore cooperating with the health authorities' teams can also lead to improved service developments and greater flexibility. Within generic teams, specialisation does occur but this usually means someone in the team taking an interest in people with SLD while priority within the team as a whole remains in childcare and family work. In such settings, service developments may be assisted by a specialist worker outside the team who has responsibility for developing services, and assisting generic teams by providing advice and expertise.

Turning now to consider the services that may be provided by a local authority social services department, a life span approach will be used.

Birth

- support through advice from social worker (available throughout life);
- parents may be counselled about the child with SLD as an integral part of the family;
- reception into care where parents who are unable to care for their child may lead to the use of adoption and fostering services;

Under five-years-old

- assistance in caring for the child by the provision of family aide and respite care in a foster or residential home, or attendance at a day nursery;
- advice on benefits (throughout life);
- provision of aids and adaptations (throughout life);
- advice on difficult behaviour;

School

- assessment under the 1981 Education Act;
- one can expect involvement from the child health service, health visitors, therapy service, educational psychologist as well as social worker;

2–19-years-old

- assistance at home by family aides, respite care, and so on; a child may still be received into care or local authority accommodation if the parents are unable to cope;
- liaison with school and attendance at meetings with parents;

Leaving school

- introduction to adult respite care in a hostel or other accommodation;
- arrangement for post school occupation at a local authority day care resource in community education, or whatever appears to

meet the young person's best interests. Full or part time employment may also be considered;

- fostering may be available from foster parents;
- assistance with caring by family aide, if parents can no longer cope or to help provide 'independence' for person with SLD;
- preparation of a long-term plan for individuals;
- provision of accommodation in own home with support, or in a flat or home with minimum support, or in group accommodation, or in a residential home;
- continued responsibility at the death of a person with a SLD.

These lists are not exhaustive and obviously there are other provisions; for example social workers may offer advice, assistance, carry out assessments, locate resources, advocate and negotiate on behalf of people with SLD and/or their families – at any time during this life cycle. Parents may refer themselves or be referred by others, and some social work teams are proactive rather than simply reacting to referrals. This means visiting parents who come to the team's notice and who have had no previous contact with a social worker.

In addition to the social services provided by the local authority, there are a number of other services which complement these. The roles of GPs, health visitors and community nurses are extremely important in the referral process. It is often at this stage that many parents fail to be referred to other agencies, which results in a denial of resources and support services. Sometimes crucial months, or even years, are lost as a child with a severe learning difficulty remains undetected, especially during the pre-school years. This, in itself, has been responsible for parents being subjected to unnecessary distress; they are expected to respond 'appropriately' when their child is suddenly asked to attend a special school for children with learning difficulties. Such an experience is very traumatic for parents who up until then had thought their child to be normal.

Six families in this study clearly represented the above comments which indicates both the apparent lack, of information on resources, and the need for a more integrated approach by all services who are responsible for providing support, advice, counselling and financial help. It should be understood that many of the comments made by parents about social workers in this study are also consistent with their feelings towards other caring agencies.

Throughout this account of services from the local authority it is assumed that the services are ethnically sensitive and that information about the various service areas is easily accessible. The rest of this chapter will illustrate how this assumption is often only notional; although it is hoped to hold true for Asian parents of a child or young adult with SLD, my study has painted a very negative picture. All of the services outlined in the life span approach are significantly reduced in their frequency and range to Asian families, and there is often little effort to change services so that they reflect the changing needs of a multicultural, multiracial society.

Asian parents have the same needs as other carers; they experience anxieties, frustration, helplessness and isolation in the same way as their White carer counterparts but, potentially, all on a deeper level because of the added ingredient of racism – personal, cultural and institutional. In spite of the similarities which exist between them in bringing up a disabled child, the opportunity to articulate their needs to service providers has been limited for those who have tried to get through; their needs have been misunderstood or not heard. The following paragraphs report some of the problems reported by Asian parents about their situation in general and their difficulties of obtaining information.

In an article in the newsletter *Carelink* (Issue 3), Jangit Uppal of the ICAN Asian Family Support Centre in Smethwick wrote:

'Bringing up a handicapped child can be a frustrating and lonely affair. Most mothers have no social life whatsoever and long periods of confinement in the home lead to an increasing isolation and loneliness. Many Asian mothers are linguistically and physically isolated from access to services and knowledge about them; some women are very unsure of what is expected of them in the UK to fulfil their role as mothers and their experience of traditional healing is hard to fit in with NHS orthodoxy on disabilities. Some are very young and inexperienced as parents, have very little in common with their white neighbours and miss the link and support offered within the extended family.'

The situation described by Jangit Uppal was borne out in the course of this research. The interview extract at the beginning of the book depicts the kind of situation experienced by many of the Asian parents interviewed in this research. Such feelings were made worse when they became aware of the range of services which could have helped them, but which they had not been informed about. When one considers the situation of the young mother above it is not surprising that some parents did not know where their social services area office is located or how to contact their allocated social worker should a problem arise. As one interviewee reported, 'He comes to see us but we don't contact him, I have the phone number somewhere I think, but we can't contact him because we don't know his address'. Others did not know how to contact a social worker, or even whether they were entitled to do so: 'Are you sure I can have a social worker? I don't want to cause any problems. My daughter often wets the bed and dirties her clothes, do you think I could get some help with that?'

Most referrals were made in response to a desperate need for advice, and parents relied upon the help of family, health visitors, school teachers or family friends, to contact the social services on their behalf. Without help from one of these sources, most probably these families would remain without the support and help to which they were entitled, and without the benefits they had legitimate claim to. When explanations were given about various benefits such as the Invalidity Care Allowance, Mobility Allowance and so on, Asian parents were unsure as to whether they were receiving these benefits or not. Attendance Allowance was another untapped financial resource which some parents were entitled to claim but had not done so. There was also some confusion about the role of the DSS and social services; there was a general impression that they were both the same agency and this tended to generate a lot of unnecessary misunderstanding and confusion.

One area of concern for parents in this study was the lack of information about their child's disability and how this led them to feel anxious and unsure about their child's future; how could they cater adequately for their child's needs if they were not aware of the extent of the disability? Several parents requested regular counselling and early support. Information on voluntary organisations and benefit appeals was definitely needed. Many parents did not know about family aides, home helps, laundry services and charitable trusts which help families caring for a handicapped child.

Perhaps the single most important point in this area, however, was the lack of information and knowledge about fostering and respite care. Social workers are particularly concerned that Asian parents do not take up these services; because of the low take up it is assumed that Asian parents use the networking in the Asian community which operates an 'informal type' of respite care. In the same context some social workers also used this assumption to reinforce the stereotype that formal respite care is seen by Asian parents as unacceptable because it implies that parents are incapable and incompetent to look after their handicapped child. This negative feeling about respite care and fostering was indeed expressed by a few of the parents interviewed, but such feelings are also experienced in the White community and should not be taken as representative of all Asian families with handicapped children. Negative feelings towards fostering and respite care often reflect a lack of understanding by Asian parents of the nature of a particular service; most did not know what was involved in respite care and fostering.

For those parents who had been using the service, there were problems with terminology: for example the words 'respite care' misled parents to assume that the care service was involuntary rather than voluntary. This simple misunderstanding led them to believe that if they agreed to this service, their child would be taken away from them and into care indefinitely.

Aside from problems with the correct interpreting and translating of attitudes about services, there were problems also of providing suitable food, communicating in the mother tongue, providing appropriate carers, and respecting cultural and religious needs – needs which are now being addressed adequately in the discussion of respite care generally. However, this is not true of all local authorities; some have adopted policies and made special provision for minority ethnic clients. Yet even in these cases parents often did not know about services because of a failure to publicise them effectively. Thus, parents unnecessarily experienced difficulties in obtaining some services, especially respite care (in their own homes, with another family or in a short-stay home), day care (with childminders, nurseries, playgroups, and so on), and foster parents.

Fostering has tended to be assumed to be demeaning to the Asian community by some White professionals. This is a myth which supports the justification used to explain low take-up of this service. As discussed earlier, fostering on an informal basis does take place in the Asian community. It is perceived by many as a religious duty, and it is a major responsibility and a major concern for all. However, in spite of this positive attitude, many prospective Asian foster parents are reluctant to be registered with social services because of the bureaucratic process this entails such as the assessment and training procedures involved and the lengthy interviews of family members and siblings. For those local authorities who have 'same race' policies which have required an aggressive recruitment campaign for more foster parents from the Asian community, expectations have been high while the response from the Asian community has been disappointingly low. One should not be disheartened by this response, and the objectives should be regarded as long-term rather than short-term. It is important to remember that the size of the problem of disability in the Asian community is only beginning to become apparent and that information in this area needs to be improved. Furthermore, the criteria appropriate to the role of fostering officers making assessments about prospective Asian foster parents need to ensure that an understanding of child-rearing practices, and cultural and religious patterns are held and recognised. If the take-up for any service is low, the blame should not be put on the target group; rather, an examination of the service should be carried out and monitored, consultation with the Asian community should be increased, and enough time should be allowed to get the service right.

Education was another area in which little information existed to provide Asian parents with a good grounding of knowledge about their child's educational needs and opportunities. It seemed that a unilateral professional decision was the norm and that there was little scope for parent involvement in the decision-making process. Choice of schools, assessments and statementing were often unclear and, because of the problems of communication, some children were being incorrectly assessed and placed in inappropriate schools, or adults were being placed in day centres for the wrong reasons. As the dialogue was only in English, parents were unsure about the explanations given to justify the accuracy of the assessments. In addition any opportunities to question these decisions were difficult to prompt as parents did not understand either the reasons why certain proposals were being made about their child's education, or that they had a right to ask for information and query or challenge decisions. In some cases parents were signing papers which they did not understand because they were in English. It is obvious that such difficulties result in extra pressure on parents who are struggling to meet the special needs of their child in the best way they can.

It is important to improve information in this area, especially with reference to the assessments, statements of special educational needs and reviews under Section 5 of the 1981 Education Act. The Parents' Charter on *Children with Special Needs* (DES, 1992) underlines the importance of parents working in partnership with professionals during assessment and understanding their rights to contribute to the statement and to use appeal procedures if they are unhappy with the provision proposed. It is not enough to have information translated into Asian languages and to feel that this is the only way to improve knowledge of services among Asian families with children with special needs. The terminology used in the leaflets, booklets and so on should ensure that the translation does not distort the intended meaning of words such as 'care'. For example, this may imply imposed care rather than voluntary care which represents a choice made by the parents concerned. For those Asian parents who are illiterate, perhaps there could be a medium of information which carries the message in pictorial form.

All information produced should be easily grasped by the Asian community in terms of language, content and subject matter. Ideally, a support and counselling surgery operated by a bi-lingual worker could do a lot to provide Asian parents with information and knowledge about education, health, social services, and the contribution of the voluntary sector. It is not sufficient just to inform people about what is available; parents need to be in contact with someone who understands their needs and who can give them the support they require to assist them in arranging to receive the benefits and services to which they are entitled.

Signpost

Most importantly, parents should be given support both at the services stage and at the emotional level. Parents must feel confident in approaching the services so that they may participate comfortably in caring for their child with various service providers. Honesty and positive critism must be applied so as to reduce high expectations and create a relationship based on practical, realistic and attainable social work interventions.

When giving information, more emphasis and priority should be given to providing equal access to information and services, particularly for those parents who are linguistically, culturally and religiously different from White clients. Discrimination may be unconscious, but will continue to exist unless the effort is made to challenge it. Asian parents require reassurance that the needs of their disabled child are important, and that, where there are difficulties in communicating the needs of their child to various authorities, provisions will be made to assist them.

5. Communication: addressing the issues

In any commentary about the Asian community the language and cultural barriers are often highlighted as the main factors leading social agencies to operate ineffectively in their dealings with those clients whose first language is not English. Communication between workers and such client groups is often considered to be difficult and such difficulties may sometimes reinforce and justify already well-formed preconceived attitudes towards the Asian community. Poor communication is also the basis from which misunderstanding breeds and alienation evolves.

Communication is the cornerstone of dialogue and social exchange; without it one feels inadequate and helpless. Within the framework of social worker and health service liaison, it is the only means by which one may prepare and respond to clients' needs adequately. A fruitful exchange is used to indicate the amount of understanding achieved between client and worker, and the realistic provision of services this may warrant. On the other hand, where communication is poor or has broken down an atmosphere of stress and confusion is created, presenting feelings of anxiety for both client and worker. Here the dialogue needed to establish rapport and trust becomes nullified and difficulty arises in assessing the needs of the client. For social workers and health workers this type of situation is commonplace when dealing with the Asian community, and there is an acceptance that preconceived attitudes toward this client group may result in a 'play on the language barrier' to invalidate any source of assistance they were unable to offer. The assumption that Asian people cannot speak English has important ramifications in terms of appropriate service delivery, counselling, information about aids and adaptations, special schools, respite care, welfare rights and access to many other services.

The problems Asian parents encounter with workers from the caring professions because of the language barrier have been discussed in detail elsewhere. In the remainder of this short chapter, I hope to move away from the rhetoric of the communication block, and focus on practical ways to reduce and subsequently erode the apparently 'stubborn' language barrier.

Communication does not occur solely at a verbal level: in order to understand others from different racial, linguistic, cultural or religious background, knowledge about the norms, beliefs and values of unfamiliar groups needs to be improved and monitored. Verbal communication, although important, should not be regarded as crucial to a successful dialogue and should be reinforced by emphasis on using non-verbal cues. This point is often forgotten and therefore avenues which may be followed to rectify faults in communication are not used or recognised. Many local authorities faced with serving a minority population where language difficulties are extreme have attempted to solve the problem by appointing interpreters, bi-lingual staff, and even teaching Urdu and Punjabi to White staff members. However, in the present financial climate there is often insufficient scope for developing these particular initiatives; so where do we go from here? The answer is to interpret 'communication' within a framework which acknowledges the importance of three interlocking systems:

- community;
- interpreters;
- interviewing skills.

These three should be used as the principal components needed in improving a two-way dialogue of exchange between two people where the English language is not shared. Developing the right approach in these three areas will assist the application and administration of the skills required to work with the Asian community as a client group.

Community

Having established that one's values and beliefs will be different from those of the client group, the following checklist demonstrates a number of ways which can ensure a better understanding and credibility with the Asian community.

- Check the diversity and range of religious and cultural practices which exist within the Asian community, familiarise yourself with them and learn to understand and respect them.
- Find out the number of languages spoken and the dialects used, especially the language your client feels most comfortable with.
- Arrange to meet and consult with members of the different Asian minority groups and use these meetings as a foundation for a forum on problems and issues of concern to the Asian community.
- Establish credibility with the Asian community by making visits as frequently as possible, perhaps attending events held by community organisations.
- Always go prepared, and be realistic about what you can offer them and clear about what you can achieve.
- Remember that any approach by a White organisation may initially be viewed with suspicion so take a long-term rather than a short-term view of one's objectives.
- Be patient and open-minded; do not be afraid to ask questions about areas you are unfamiliar with and unsure about how to respond to appropriately, without being unintentionally offensive.
- Observe gender issues and question the appropriateness of a male worker visiting a female Asian group or vice versa.
- Observe religious and cultural events and organise meetings around these important days.
- Be relaxed in your approach. Be sensitive to the discrimination the clients experience in their everyday lives. Tell them that you are ignorant of their needs and need to find a correct means to identify them, so that assistance may be given which will be more useful, and culturally and religiously acceptable.
- Make use of Asian community organisations to set up advice surgeries, thereby creating greater access to information about services and benefits.

In meeting with members from any community which is different to one's own, a little preparatory work and foresight can help tremendously and may be the main difference between getting it right or wrong. Increasing one's familiarity with the Asian community is beneficial for both parties as it can provide a good introductory basis for a much needed consultative framework to identify common needs and common areas of concern.

Interpreters

Help or hindrance

Where communication difficulties are encountered the use of an interpreting or translating agency often comes into play. In the majority of cases interpreters are used on a voluntary basis; few are employed by social services and this in itself is seen to reflect the lack of concern and valuation placed on the important role such a service can offer to clients. There has been much debate about the reliability of information given through interpreters, and the low professional and organisational status attached to them, their role being seen as sub-professional by other workers who fail to acknowledge their usefulness in transcending the communication barrier.

Whatever the reasons for or against using interpreters, it is widely recognised by the Asian community that they have a right of access to information, and that it is the responsibility of the social services and other statutory departments to ensure such access is equal and non-discriminatory. If this involves employing interpreters then let it be so; but what must be avoided is a sub-standard service rather than a service which has been well-planned and thought-through.

In this section we will look at the case of interpreters as a help or a hindrance; it is hoped that the important role interpreters have to play will be shown, together with the ways in which they may be a positive help. The frequency of the use of an interpreter will depend on the type of relationship sought between client and worker, and the subject matter of the interview. For example, social workers giving advice on welfare rights express a desire for mutual rational understanding rather than emotional contact. This kind of advice is easier to communicate through an interpreter, especially when it is desperately sought and highly valued. Interviews concerned with emotional responses and reactions can be difficult because the interpersonal skills needed to allow the discourse to develop productively are often unfamiliar to the interpreter – and the interpreter's level of skill in this area is often very difficult to check.

Interpretation may be considered useful for obtaining background information; but counselling and emotional relationships in general are difficult or impossible to carry out through the medium of interpreters.

It is not the object of this section to look in detail at the controversial area of interpreting and translating services. However, it is vital to acknowledge that interpreters are used ineffectively when low priority is given to them by social workers. Their role is sometimes considered a luxury for the clients rather than as a necessity for professional practice. Among some social workers there is an overriding feeling that there should be some compulsory general education about Asian cultures so that they can begin to appreciate differences and recognise needs. However, little reference is made to the employed interpreters as a resource for providing cultural information – a resource which is freely available and on hand.

Why use a professional interpreter?

Using interpreters can help to break down isolation, but to utilise them productively, certain guidelines should be observed:

- Social workers individually may have very low numbers of Asian clients, that is only a small proportion of their caseload will be Asian. Because of this they may not perceive communication with Asians to be a serious problem.
- One of the functions of being an interpreter may be to work with Asian communities to develop more awareness of demands on social services. This suggests that interpreters could be beneficial to the Asian community in providing knowledge of social services and feedback of responses.
- It is wholly unacceptable to use children to interpret, or to expect clients who have language difficulties to bring their own community interpreter.
- The need to recognise the unsuitability of child members of the family for translating purposes; this is unethical and unprofessional.
- Interpreting by family members should be avoided because of the possible biases and power relationships within the family.
- Make sure clients and interpreters are matched as far as possible in terms of linguistic and religious background, to avoid the risk of inter-racial conflict.

The interpreter–social worker relationship

In any interpretation and translation of materials or spoken words a very high level of interpreting skills is required and these skills include: fluent communication; ability to engage clients directly while speaking as directed by someone else; sensitivity and interpersonal skills; a calm and non-threatening personality; the capacity to offer comfort in discussing personal and emotional topics. The skills required of a good social worker are no less taxing. Both interpreter and social worker need a special sympathy when working with Asian clients and this suggests that it is vital for both parties to be aware of the other's skills and limitations if they are to succeed in achieving the desired goal.

When communication breaks down between them this can result in the following problems:

- Social workers may feel excluded if they feel the interpreter is becoming too involved with the client.
- Limited involvement with the client promotes a mechanical and stilted interview.
- The need for interpreters to explain unfamiliar words, concepts and procedures; this may exclude the social worker who may begin to feel de-skilled.
- The interpreter may feel it culturally inappropriate to translate particular language, for example language which is abusive, or language related to sexual behaviour.
- Social workers inevitably become dependent on the interpreters to carry out their tasks. Even non-verbal tasks are culture bound and the social worker may feel that his or her cultural ignorance is all too apparent.
- There may be barriers between the Asian client and the interpreter; these must be respected and if possible overcome, for example matters of religion, sex and social class.

In order to avoid these problems, it is essential to prepare an action plan based on a review of the partnerships actually and potentially embedded in the interview.

Social work, at its best, involves the generation of a sense of partnership between workers and clients (albeit modified by social and structural factors). The presence of an interpreter – particularly one of the same race as the client but not of the worker – creates the risk that the worker-client partnership will be replaced by an interpreter-client partnership from which the worker feels (or even, at worst, seeks) separation. The action plan therefore should be concerned to promote the necessity of a worker-interpreter partnership (including mutual professional understanding and respect) in the context of the essential ongoing partnership between worker and client.

The action plan

- Interpreters and social workers should insist on mutual briefing sessions before the interview with clients and extra time should be allowed for de-briefing afterwards.
- Social workers should ensure that the interpreter is well versed in the information needed to be obtained from the interview and the importance of confidentiality.
- Check for compatibility in the use of language and other matching variables such as religion, sex and so on to create a comfortable interviewing atmosphere.
- The professionalism of the interpreter should be respected.
- To provide an effective service, staff using the interpreters need training on how to prepare, speak through and discuss events with the interpreter after the interview.
- Extensive care should be taken to ensure that all information will be kept confidential. The risk of leakage by interpreters of confidential and delicate matters is a very real fear among the Asian community, and should be addressed with sensitivity.

Interviewing skills

So far we have discussed how developing access procedures to Asian communities and using interpreters may be helpful. Little attention has been paid to the problems involved when English is available as a common language but, in spite of this, for some reason Asian clients and their social workers find themselves at cross-purposes. This is particularly apparent in the home interview when the cultural etiquette practised by Asian clients is not known to social workers or is misunderstood.

Since communication is power, redressing the balance of cross-cultural discrimination is essential. However, one cannot simply be taught these social conventions; moreover an increased awareness of them is needed because of the misinterpretations which may arise due to different modes of vocabulary and syntax used by varying English-speakers. Social workers and health workers who feel they are tolerant sometimes find that there are hidden ways in which they discriminate unconsciously. Sometimes they feel that their systems are fair and non-discriminatory even though most probably they create and perpetuate precisely the kinds of prejudice and stereotyping that we are all interested in destroying.

Any attempts to redress the balance and apply pressure to change systems will always outweigh the risks and dangers involved in ignoring their defects. Interviewing schedules and patterns of dialogue for professionals who wish to avoid failure, mutual frustration and shared mis-understanding, should attempt to incorporate the following components of a good interview.

A good interview

- An Asian client may not share the same expectations and assumptions about what is appropriate in terms of behaviour or response in this situation. It would be useful here to check what these are by consulting with other members of the appropriate Asian community to establish an 'etiquette of decorum'.
- Be prepared to state your own assumptions about what is required or customary. Explain clearly about the necessary production of certificates, for verification of date of birth for example. Remember that on the Indian sub-continent births, deaths, and marriages are not always registered and, therefore, too much emphasis on the need to produce such documents may cause undue stress.
- Be careful not to attract suspicion by asking at an inappropriate time about your client's immigration status and how many people are living in the house; this may be perceived as threatening and racist.
- Use very explicit questions and rely on stress and intonation to carry your meaning. Don't offend your client by speaking very slowly and loudly; rely on interpersonal, non-verbal skills to complement your speech.
- Remember that you probably do not share the same systems for expressing tone of voice and emphasis, so allow time to develop your listening skills to focus on verbal differences.
- Talk openly about discrimination; this may prompt your clients to explain some of their reactions, feelings and expectations which need to be acknowledged.

- Listen until they have completely finished; important points may have been left towards the end of their answers. In addition, if you do not share the same ways of explaining things and giving information, it is fatal to switch off, jump to conclusions or interrupt.
- To avoid unintentional discrimination resulting from different ways of using English, allow extra time to get to know the other person.
- Be aware of gender differences – it may or may not be appropriate to shake an Asian lady's hand, or to sit alone with her.
- Establish the correct name of your client and be careful not to pronounce it in an abbreviated form.
- Refrain from using Asian words that you have picked up, especially on your first visit; Asian clients may find this patronising and offensive.

Signpost

In this chapter I have tried to address communication in the context of community, interpreters and interviewing skills. The lists provided to help reduce the mis-communication experienced by Asian parents in this study are obviously not exhaustive. It is hoped that they will be used as a possible signpost for developing and adapting an individual approach by all practitioners in the caring professions. 'Translation is at best an echo' indicates the way towards a new type of service delivery which at no point fails to recognise the difficulties involved in implementing these strategic patterns effectively.

Social service departments, through experience, have learnt much (and in some cases little) about their attempts to break down the barriers between their workers and the Asian communities. Perhaps the most important lesson is to accept that there are no short-cuts or easy answers. The barriers will only finally be broken down through careful thought and planning, and an increase in personnel resources devoted to the Asian communities. Communication is only one of the issues to be resolved and understood, but it is the beginning of any desire to shape and reformulate services for the Asian community.

6. The way forward – Positive recommendations to improve service provision to the Asian family with a disabled child

In this book the problems that Asian parents encounter when dealing with the local authority have been documented. Similarly the concerns that social workers have in meeting the needs of the Asian population have also been expressed. It would have been inappropriate to highlight problems without offering ways in which they may be overcome or resolved.

Through this research and throughout my professional career I have often found that, in some cases, very little money is required in order to make services more positive and welcoming to the Asian client. In some instances the changes are far from dramatic, requiring a little thought and improved communication skills. For example, when someone is visiting the Social Service Area Office for the first time, the role of the receptionist is a crucial one. It is at this point of reference that one is made to feel comfortable or completely alienated. Unfortunately most research indicates that it is often the first contact of the receptionist which creates a snowballing effect of misunderstanding, alienation and the experience of racism for non-White clients; these feelings are further exacerbated when a common language is also absent.

Reception skills are extremely important especially for minority ethnic clients, where the attitude perceived here normally sets the pattern of perceived events for the rest of their contact with social services. A simple training course in communication and interpersonal skills can do a lot to reduce the occurrence of this damaging stage.

The following recommendations suggest that the local authority, health authority and voluntary sector should respond to anyone with a disability as a person first, with the disability being seen as an added dimension. Cultural and religious factors should be a major concern if local authorities are going to provide a service which is not only accessible but appropriate, and which ensures an improved and effective service delivery and a better quality of health and social care for Asian people with a mental or physical handicap.

General aims

Background information

Appropriate services can only be provided if each local authority is fully informed about the nature of the community which it is serving.

Residents from the New Commonwealth and Pakistan in the UK number approximately 2-4 million. Detailed analysis of the patterns of settlement and ethnicity in each local authority should be encouraged so that the provision of services can begin to match the proportional level of the minority ethnic community. Using umbrella terms to break down the minority ethnic population into African-Caribbean, Indian sub-continent and so on is insufficient.

Information is also needed about language, culture and religion; for example, the Muslim community includes the majority of the Pakistani and Bangladeshi community with some Indians, East Africans, Asians, Arabs, Malaysians and West Indians. Although Islam may be the common denominator, language and culture will be wholly different and may vary from community to community and even between individuals from the same racial background.

Integration versus segregation

Britain is now a multiracial, multicultural and multilingual society and this has to be acknowledged before any effective strategies can be evolved.

The responsibility of providing for the Asian community should not be seen as different or separate from that of the indigenous White population. It is unhelpful to discuss the social welfare of the Asian community within the framework of 'host' and 'immigrant' communities for this may have the effect of marginalising the needs of the Asian community instead of integrating them within mainstream provision. Furthermore, the specific needs of the Asian community should not be seen as 'additional work', a burden or a problem.

Provision should not be undertaken as an additional approach but should be an integrated part of planning.

Research

Research should be seen as an integral part of service delivery to the minority ethnic community and account should be taken of socio/ economic and environmental factors rather than over generalised ethnic differences.

As Pearson has indicated (1991), research is needed not simply into imported, exotic and infectious diseases, but into the sensitivity of service response to minority ethnic groups. She suggests how some recent research has ignored the socio-economic and environmental causes of ill-health and has concentrated instead on 'over-generalised' stereotyped socio/ethnic factors. For example, Bundey (1990) linked the incidence of prenatal mortality and mental subnormality with consanguinity, while Barker (1984) and Pocock (1975) linked absenteeism among Asians with the extended family, ignoring their working conditions. Simplistic explanations based on cultural difference may in some cases divert attention from real explanations, as prevalent in the inadequacy of service provision to the Asian community.

For example, the low uptake of respite services by Asian parents with a disabled child may be attributable to factors such as inadequate translations, the reluctance of parents to have their daughter cared for by male carers, and a lack of knowledge and experience of social services.

Communication

A qualitative and valuable service which enhances sensitivity to Asian clients' needs depends on the absence or presence of an effective communication system. This is true of the whole range of relationships in the local and health authority framework; for example:

- Within the context of diagnosis there is the need to take complex case histories and understand symptomatic details.
- Treatment instructions about drugs, diet and so on need to be clarified and clearly understood.
- Assessment of a child's educational ability and the procedure of statementing needs to be communicated in detail.
- Information about good practice, services available, and the rights of parents should be offered with support and guidance.
- Opportunities should be made available for parents to cross-check that they understand and to avoid misinterpretation. This cross-

checking should be extended to the professional so that the level of one's communication skills can be monitored in any given situation.

As far as possible a comprehensive interpreting service should be provided. Attention should be given to proper training for both interpreter and user so that expectations on both sides do not clash.

Using children or other members of the family to interpret and cope with complex information, nuances of meaning and personal details is unsatisfactory and may result in information being wrongly interpreted to the detriment of the client concerned. All interpreters, advocated or link-workers should understand the subtleties of meaning related to feelings and cultural differences as well as to medical terminology. Interpersonal skills and the role of non-verbal communication in networking an effective dialogue should be incorporated into all training activities for staff, especially those working in the reception areas.

Due to the link between inappropriate service provision and communication on the one hand and low uptake of services on the other, all service providers should evaluate the appropriateness of their present service and conduct campaigns designed to inform the Asian community of the service available, linked with out-reach workers and community support work.

Furthermore special efforts should be made to make use of minority ethnic press and organisations to highlight issues, inform communities about particular services, and ensure that positive campaigns of recruitment and employment are appropriately targeted.

The Race Relations Act (1976): employment and training
Where appropriate, full use should be made of the positive action provisions of the 1976 Race Relations Act, especially in employment, an area in which discrimination rears its ugly head in the recruitment field as well as in the area of service provision.

One of the most important sections of this Act is Section 20 which make it unlawful for anyone concerned with the provision of goods, facilities or services to the public to discriminate on racial grounds by refusing or deliberately omitting to provide them. This discrimination may be direct (less favourable treatment) or indirect (applying a requirement or condition which has a disproportionately adverse affect on a particular racial group which cannot be justified).

With reference to employment, section 5(2)(d) of the Race
Relations Act (1976) allows the specific appointment of a member of
a particular racial group where the holder of the job concerned can
only be met by someone who shares similar language, cultural and
religious understanding.

Where Black people are under-represented in the workforce,
particularly at management level, Sections 37 and 38 may be used to
increase the numbers of Black employees. Furthermore, they are
useful in reinforcing positive action training, and encouragement
where members of a certain racial group are under-represented in a
specific area of the work force. This is irrespective of significant
Black service users.

The local authority should use the provision of the Race Relations
Act of 1976 accordingly and register openly its commitment to
combat racism and to promote equal opportunities in employment
and service provision.

So far, many of the points discussed have been placed in a more
generalised context of the needs of the Asian community as a whole.
Concentration will now be given to recommendations on service
delivery to the Asian disabled client and on the special consideration
this obviously requires.

Specific objectives

Training

This section discusses training as one of the many avenues in which
one may improve services. However, it does not necessarily place
training at the top of the hierarchy for effecting change. Moreover, it
may only be constructive if it is dealt with as a structural process in a
strategy for developing better services.

Policy implementation used to identify gaps within service
provision must take prevalence over training as it will be the main
device upon which training may be a part. Again, training is often
used as a means to change attitudes; since this is not the reality, nor
the purpose of training, policies must be drawn up and adhered to,
which construct training packages, which will seek to evaluate
services and identify good practice, building in emphasis on personal
strategies of action, as well as departmental. The integral role that
the management plays within this context is often overlooked,
especially in the consultation process. For training to be effective, it

is essential that managers have a clear understanding of the objectives behind any training programme. There must be mutual cooperation between managers and their training staff, and an equal respect for trainers and their commitment to facilitate anti-racist and anti-discriminatory practice in their training. Where training has been discussed within the above objectives, the following recommendations may be useful:

- All training should integrate relevant race issues and a consistent anti-racist approach throughout all the activities of the social services training section when dealing with special needs.
- Emphasis should be placed on perceiving Asian parents with a disabled child as encountering and expressing the same concerns and anxieties as non-Asian parents. But here it is important to understand and recognise the cultural and religious dimensions which will be significant in achieving a more sensitive approach.
- Depending on the range of resources available, training programmes will differ; an example of a recommended training programme would be as follows:
  - to examine the quality of practitioners' current practice, and then to establish what is needed;
  - input and consultation from parents and community projects should be encouraged as far as possible; this will help service providers to develop a clearer picture of gaps in service provision to the Asian community.
  - consultation between professionals working across various disciplines, such as social services, health, education, housing department and the voluntary sector. This can assist in developing strategies, changes in practices and so on, in order to create a service which is appropriate and sensitive to the needs of Asian families.
  - as far as possible, one should include Black trainers or Black trainers with a disability, on any training in this area.

Areas which could be included in a training programme include:

- How services are planned both departmentally and across disciplines, identifying gaps in service provision.
- Development of a policy for monitoring services.
- What is good practice when working with White families?
- What is the common core of good practice irrespective of cultural factors?

- What are the unfamiliar/unknown areas for practitioners?
- What are their fears/anxieties about working with Asian families?
- What problems or misunderstandings arise?
- What are the cultural stereotypes?
- What are the attitudes of Asian families towards the services?
- What are the experiences and expectations of families with a disabled child?
- In what ways do they differ from the experiences of White or other cultural groups/families?
- What other relevant considerations, additional requirements, or resources are needed?
- What are the pros and cons of specialist provision compared with an integrated service?
- How can current practices be improved and developed?
- What are the implications for service planners?
- Are families with children with disabilities directly involved in training events for professionals?

Working parties

Small discussion groups should be facilitated to address the points listed above. Such forums are also useful to keep up-to-date with changes in practice and to provide support/advice to practitioners when difficulties arise.

Working parties can also be useful for training meetings in which a topic can be chosen for detailed discussion, for example, the diversity of Asian cultures and religions. Members from various communities could be invited to talk about their community and the implication of its cultural/religious components when meeting needs.

Other issues

Aside from training, there are many other measures one can adopt at a more personal level which will help to secure a more positive and active relationship with other clients.

- **The parent practitioner relationship**

Asian parents should be encouraged to become more involved in the decision-making processes which affect the present and future welfare of their disabled child.

Practitioners can improve this situation by gaining the confidence of the parents through allowing extra time during the initial contact stages. This can be essential to paving the way for a collaborative relationship. Information giving should be clarified by feedback in both directions so that misinterpretation by client and worker can be avoided.

Opportunities for taking part in cultural groups and activities should be fostered; this may serve a double purpose in that parents can meet with their social workers on a more informal basis and social workers can benefit from greater cultural understanding.

The most important aspect of this relationship is for both client and worker to feel at ease with each other. It is far easier to discuss one's problems with someone you feel to be sympathetic rather than with someone who is not.

Problems about information, about services, the rights of parents, the system of appeals on benefits and educational assessments, aids and adaptations are all areas in which clients' knowledge is often limited. A good relationship between parent and social worker offers one way in which these issues can be explored.

● **Open day across services**

In order to improve communication between service providers and Asian families, open days at the various departments concerned with children with special needs can be extremely constructive. These could be one way of addressing the information gap and it constitutes a statement of positive intent by service providers by indicating a commitment to improve service delivery and to develop a more ethnically sensitive service.

The provision of services

● **Short term care and fostering**
  The needs here are for:
  – a long term policy for the recruitment of more Asian parents;
  – training to educate parents about the nature of the respite care service and its utility to them;
  – training of carers who are unfamiliar with the cultural, and religious and dietary needs of an Asian child;
  – where a policy exists to provide Asian children in care with the diet of their choice and with a sense of religious/cultural security, this should be known to both parents and practitioners;

– as far as possible, female carers should be provided for female residents and this provision should be emphasised to Asian parents who have a daughter with a mental handicap.

• **Specialist posts**

Full and part-time Asian consultants should be actively involved in developing service and appropriate training modules. Advocates and link workers should be appointed to liaise between parent and client where a communication problem exists. Such appointments should have access to future promotions by social work training courses and so on. Part-time Asian counsellors should operate counselling surgeries in Asian organisations and should assist in initiating self-help groups for Asian parents with a child with a disability.

• **Further recommendations**

– All staff working with Asian families should have consistent anti-racist training which should be regularly reviewed and updated.
– The introduction of ethnic monitoring to assist in analysing services, employment opportunities and research needs in respect of specific issues of concern.
– The recruitment of more bilingual minority ethnic staff.
– Information to be translated into appropriate minority languages; pictorial information and ideas to be introduced to ensure information is getting across to those who are both illiterate in English and in their own language.
– Local authorities and health authorities must be seen to take account of minority ethnic needs when assessing priorities for community care.
– Specialist career officers need to be made fully aware of the particular circumstances and needs of minority ethnic persons with disabilities.
– All local authorities should take up their responsibilities to provide adequate and appropriate service provision to persons from minority ethnic groups under the Race Relations Act 1976.

The Children Act 1989

Children's services over the last decade have become more concerned with accountability and responsibility to children in particular and to society at large.

With increasing reported cases of child abuse and consistent media coverage of poor practice in local authorities and health authorities public pressure has resulted in the government taking firmer steps to keep children services 'in check'.

The Children Act 1989 is a revolutionary piece of legislation which effectively attempts to maintain the child's interests as paramount and to acknowledge the role of the family, local authorities and public law in any assessment of the child needs. While implementation of the aims and objectives of the Children Act are extremely complicated and delicate there is a growing concern among the local authorities to ensure that the needs of Asian children in care are given adequate and responsive services.

The recommendations cited so far in this chapter to develop and improve services to this client group go some way in offering positive guidelines to assist any analytical framework to enable local authorities to do this in the context of the Children Act. However, there are some specific areas where the act obviously needs further in depth considerations and this shall be addressed below.

Since this book is about disability, that part of the Children Act (children in need) which addresses it shall be discussed although much of the information will be transferable across children services as listed in the act itself.

The Children Act 1989 and 'children in need'

The Children Act 1989 consolidates the statutory basis for services provided by the local authority, and integrates old and new duties relating to children and young people with reference to the Child Care Act 1980, the National Assistance Act 1948, the NHS and Community Care Act 1990 and the various Education Acts (in particular the 1981 Education Act).

Part III of the Children Act 1989 introduces a new concept of 'children in need'. Under Sections 17-30 of the Children Act, local authorities are expected to provide a range and level of services appropriate to safeguard and promote the welfare of children in need in their area. The definition of children in need in Schedule 2,

Section 17 of the Act states that a child is regarded as 'being in need' if:

'(a) he or she is unlikely to achieve or maintain or to have the opportunity of achieving or maintaining a reasonable standard of health or development without the provision for him or her of services by a local authority under this Part of the Act.

(b) his or her health or development is likely to be significantly impaired or further impaired without the provision for him or her of services or;

(c) he or she is disabled.'

The definition of disability used in the Act is the definition used in the 1948 National Assistance Act (to ensure compatibility with other disability legislation such as the 1970 Chronically Sick and Disabled Persons Act; and the Disabled Persons Act 1986 and social security legislation). But the Department of Health Guidance on children with disabilities and the Children Act emphasise the importance of local authorities consulting with local parents and community groups to develop a working definition of disability which is appropriate and acceptable to service users and which encourages parental confidence in the role of local authorities in helping families with disabled children.

Local authorities have new duties to identify the children in need within their locality and furthermore to provide and publicise information about any service which might help them. The Children Act lays duties upon the *whole* local authority, including education, housing, recreation and leisure, to work together in the best interests of children. Health authorities also have new duties to collaborate with local authorities. Local authorities do not have to provide all the services required by children in need themselves. They may access these through other statutory or voluntary or private agencies as appropriate. The Children Act, therefore, foreshadows the community care arrangements in introducing the concept of 'care management' by the local authority. As noted elsewhere, throughout any arrangements made for children, the local authority must now take account of Section 22 5(C) of the Act, which requires that when making any decision about a child, the local authority must give 'due consideration to the child's religious persuasion, racial origin, culture and language'. This new duty combines with another new

duty to ensure that when children have to live away from natural
families, the local authority should also take steps to reunite such
children with their families and to promote contact with the family
during separation (Section 23(6) and (7) of the Act). These
provisions should ensure that the specific needs of Asian children
with disabilities are more precisely assessed and more effectively met
through a range of local services in the future.

The Children Act emphasises five important key principles in
working with children and families, namely:

- **safeguarding and promoting the welfare of children in need** –
  children whom the local authority is 'looking after' and other
  children living away from home;
- **partnership with parents** – there is a new onus on the local
  authority to try and help parents without recourse to compulsory
  powers and the courts;
- **listening to children and parents** – the local authority must now
  take due account of the wishes and feelings of children and
  families when planning or providing services;
- **the importance of families** – children should be brought up
  within their own families wherever possible and 'families' are
  redefined to include extended as well as immediate natural
  families;
- **the principle of corporate responsibility** – the local authority as a
  whole, not just social services, has new duties under the Act.

These key principles are of particular importance with regard to
duties towards children *in need*. Although the Children Act does not
specify a formal assessment process for children in need – and indeed
states that local authorities may legally assess children in need at the
same time as other relevant assessments under the 1981 Education
Act, the Chronically Sick and Disabled Persons Act or the Disabled
Persons Act – the principles listed above of listening to children and
families should ensure that assessment is seen as something more
proactive – and that the wider cultural and social needs of families
from diverse ethnic backgrounds should have a new relevance in
terms of planning for children.

Although the Children Act is also not specific about the quantity or
exact nature of provision for children in need, the local authority now
has a duty to make some form of provision with reference to:

- advice, guidance and counselling;

- occupational, social, cultural and recreational activities;
- help with transport to use services;
- assistance with holidays;
- financial and other help if appropriate.

The above include a newly defined duty to provide day care not only in terms of supervised activities for children under five but also for after-school and holiday provision for younger children. Local authorities (education as well as social services departments) have new joint duties to review day care and take account of any special needs in local communities. Respite care is covered by foster care regulations and is part of another new duty to provide 'accommodation' for children in need. Accommodation can provide respite, residential or foster care and there is a specific duty in the Act for local authorities to ensure that such accommodation is 'not unsuitable to the needs of a disabled child'. When children are accommodated by the local authority (even for short periods of respite care), there are new duties to have individual plans for every child. Such plans must reflect the views of parents and children (if able to contribute their views) and must be regularly reviewed at statutory intervals.

An important new duty on local authorities is to maintain a *Register* of children with disabilities. Registration is voluntary for parents, but a register developed in close consultation with local community groups and seen as the basis for a working relationship with social services (as well as a signpost to other services) might make a significant difference to the lives of Asian families with disabled children – many of whom receive such inadequate information on local services and are frequently not involved in planning the future shape of services to meet their special needs.

The Register of Disabled Children is quite separate to Child Protection or At Risk Registers which may also be maintained in local authorities. The Children Act introduces a new range of Court Orders to protect children who may have suffered or be suffering from harm. Great emphasis is also placed upon complaints procedures (which must have an independent element) to ensure that parents and children can make complaints if they are unhappy with local services.

Local authorities may also appoint independent visitors for children living away from home; Guardians ad litem for children going through court procedures and education supervisors for children who are having problems with education (particularly with reference to non-attendance at school). Recent court cases have also highlighted the vulnerability of children in general – and those with disabilities in particular – who are attending independent residential schools. The Children Act introduces new regulations for independent inspection of schools and, together with the various measures listed above, assumes that local authorities will take a more dynamic attitude to ensuring children's welfare. In all these different provisions, the general over-arching duty to have consideration for cultural, religious and ethnic issues will apply and the new procedures offer new opportunities to ensure that children with disabilities in the Asian communities (and their parents) to receive more culturally appropriate services.

Children living away from home
Section 20(1) of the Children Act sets out the arrangements for providing accommodation (a new term) for children who need to live away from home. Every local authority shall now provide accommodation for any child in need within their area who appears to require accommodation as a result of:

'• there being no person who has parental responsibility for him;
• his being lost or having been abandoned; or
• the person who has been caring for him being prevented (whether or not permanently, and for whatever reason) from providing him with suitable accommodation or "care".'

Before offering accommodation the local authority must ascertain the child's wishes and feelings, so far as is practicable and consistent with the child's welfare, and give them due consideration (Section 20(b)).

The Children Act offers a whole range of challenges and opportunities which need to be answered in respect to providing active care provision for Asian children. Regulations and Guidance (Volumes 3 and 5 of the Guidance) emphasise the importance of written agreements being made with children and parents or with anyone else (such as a member of the extended family) who may be looking after a child. Amongst other things, the agreement must specify:

• the purpose of the child's stay in local authority accommodation;
• arrangements for contact between child and family;

- any sharing of parental responsibility;
- on the assumption that it will usually be best for the child to return home, to make plans for such a return with all those concerned.

The local authority must now recognise new duties when providing accommodation for a child. Placements should be with a person connected with the child whenever possible – including parents, relatives or friends. Placements should be near a child's home to maintain links with local community, schools, friends and so on. Siblings should be accommodated together and – for the first time – Section 23 specifies that 'accommodation for a disabled child should not be unsuitable to the child's needs'. Accommodation may be with families or in residential settings. Schedule 2 (para 1 1(b) now requires local authorities 'to have regard to the different racial groups to which children in need in their area belong when recruiting foster parents'.

Because reunification with family is seen as of prime importance, Schedule 2, para 10(b) requires local authorities to promote contact between any separated children in need and the child's family. The authority may contribute to the costs of visits to or by children it is looking after and – if a child has little contact with friends or family – the local authority *must* appoint an independent visitor (Schedule 2, para 17). Such an independent visitor would be expected to be appropriate to the cultural or ethnic needs of the child concerned and again has a bridging role with the local community.

In implementing the Children Act we need to clarify what are the implications of race, culture, language, religion for a wide range of children's services? How can an integrated approach be developed where service providers recognise the information gap between them and the Black/Asian community and wish to reduce this? What are the implications for training of staff to incorporate the Children Act in a meaningful way to Asian children and their carers. What is the role of voluntary and community groups in ensuring effective implementation?

Implications for local authorities
The Children Act 1989 is now on the statute book and is an extremely significant political force in social policy. For the first time in child legislation specific reference has been made for local authorities to take account of a child's racial origin and ethnic and linguistic background (Section 22 (5)), religion also falls into this category).

On the surface this has important implications for social workers, and indeed for the local authority as a whole, as it will be unlawful to ignore the race, culture, language and religion of children looked after by the statutory and voluntary organisations. The Race Relations Act 1976, Section 71, reinforces this duty and should be read in conjunction with this legislation and not in isolation from it. Thus when considering the legal responsibilities of local authorities in fulfilling their duties toward children in their care, the general duty under the Race Relations Act is pertinent:

Section 71
'... it shall be the duty of every local authority to make appropriate arrangements with a view of securing that their various functions are carried out with due regard to the needs

(a) to eliminate unlawful discrimination; and
(b) to promote equality of opportunity, and good relations, between persons of different racial groups.'

One could argue that the Race Relations Act 1976, has had varying degrees of sucesses for enforcing and implementing the above within local authorities. Childcare services have been in some areas inappropriate for Asian children because of a lack of understanding regarding their language needs, culture, religion and racial backgrounds.

The Children Act in many ways will offer new opportunities to work in a positive framework with Asian children and their families.

Points to consider
A key element of the Act is to develop a notion of a partnership between families with children in need and the service providers. It sets a new and perhaps higher threshold for compulsory state intervention in family life. It also corrects the hitherto unequal contest between families (parents, children and relatives) and the state (local authorities) where there is disagreement between them over whether the state should compulsorily intervene. All of this will require local authorities to be prepared for challenges as there is a new greater opportunity to scrutinise the local authority's 'case'.

Crucial to implementing the Act is the dissemination of information. Local authorities 'must publish information about services', and since language needs are now statutory it is compulsory for local authorities to translate and interpret information on the Act and children's services in minority ethnic languages.

In addition local authorities will also need to take account of the implications for doing this, effectively. Implementation of Section 22 (5), (part 1 (3)), which refers to the child's racial origin, ethnic and linguistic background, age and sex, will need much more than translated information to improve the assessments of needs for Asian children.

The Commission for Racial Equality (CRE) through negotiation strengthened the Children Act further by requesting a new clause which places a duty on local authorities to ensure that their pool of day carers and foster carers take account of the ethnic composition of the local population. This will help to ensure that the possibility of same race placements could be exercised as of right in practice for minority ethnic children, just as it is for White children. In reference to language the CRE have stressed the importance of local authorities giving due consideration to the child's language with respect to a child it is looking after or proposing to look after.

Research by the Voluntary Organisation Liaison Council for Under Fives (VOLCUF) has shown that this could be especially important for pre-school children, who are at a crucial stage of their development. Maintenance of contact with the fluency in the mother tongue is of benefit to a child's all-round intellectual and academic progress. Being placed in an environment where a families language is spoken provides important continuity and assists both confidence and understanding.

In terms of prevention there is increasing concern that the disproportionate number of minority ethnic children in care may be indicative, in part, of cultural misunderstanding, ethno-centric value judgements or a lack of understanding, of the strengths of minority ethnic families. This has also been highlighted by the experience of Wandsworth Social Services Departments Adoption and Fostering Unit in their examination of White workers common misgivings or misconceptions about minority ethnic families.

The CRE among others agree that in accommodating a child in registered children's homes with foster carers or in day care services it should be the duty of the local authority to take account of the child's racial origin, religion, culture and language when safeguarding and promoting his/her welfare. This new duty under the

Children Act should also be extended to the criteria used in determining the reasons and decisions for taking children in to care.

What next

Now that race, culture, religion and language are on the agenda what must local authorities and other agency's do to ensure they are considered appropriately in the context of implementing the Children Act, particularly Section 22 (5).

The following model is to provide professionals with some working foundation from which to develop their own practice and the practice of their agency.

A model of good practice

- Acknowledgement of the differential power relations between professionals and clients.
- Out-reach work to identify actual or potential community based resources which may assist in meeting the needs of the client.
- Building up knowledge and understanding of the community concerned which will lead to:
  - a perception of the strengths which exist within that community;
  - a general understanding of the make-up of that community, for example, culture, religion, language, dress, diet;
  - a picture of the norms of that community;
  - a recognition of the individual nature of the client and family;
  - an acknowledgement that the needs of individual families and individual clients may vary considerably within a given community;
  - communicating to the family the workers' willingness to work on these principles, which will enable the family to nurture a positive rapport with the social worker.
- Making sure that the family is aware of the full range of services available to them, and that they have statutory rights that they should know about.
- Taking every step possible, which may include negotiations and influence with statutory and/or voluntary bodies, to provide the services identified through assessment.
- Where needs are identified but resources are 'unavailable' this should justify pressure on managers to:
  - re-appraise services;

- address resource allocation (remembering the new 'corporate duties' of the local authority);
- provide training;
- monitor provision.
- Any criticism of the services should be taken on board with a positive analysis which should lead to improvements in the service without losing credibility. This means that there should be an open complaints procedure and management commitment to actively assess and re-evaluate the issues of concern.
- An equal opportunities policy which clarifies the responsibility of the service providers to assure active and consistent anti-discriminatory practice. This should define what is expected of staff, and be modelled by senior managers and seen to work in practice.

The agency

In order for a model of good practice to be implemented it has to be supported by consistent policy and practice throughout the agency. The framework needed to achieve this is dependent upon active policy procedures, clearly drawn up and practised at senior managerial level and across the board.

Implications for the agency

- Appropriate child services can only be provided if each agency is fully informed about the nature of the community it is serving.
- Britain is now a multicultural, multiracial, multi-religious, multilingual society and this has to be acknowledged before any effective strategy can be evolved.
- Research should be seen as an integral part of service delivery to Asian children in need. Social, economic and environmental factors should be identified rather than relying on over-generalised ethnic differences.
- As far as possible a comprehensive interpreting/translation service should be provided, attention should be given to proper training for both interpreter, translator and user to avoid clash of expectations.
- Due to the link between appropriate service provision and communication on the one hand and low uptake of service, on the other, all service providers should evaluate the effectiveness of their existing services in the context of the Children Act. They

should conduct campaigns to inform the Asian community about the Act and how it affects them and their children, linked with outreach workers, and community based teams.

- Special efforts should be used to disseminate information through minority ethnic press and organisations to highlight issues, inform communities about particular services and ensure that positive campaigns of foster carers recruitment are targeted carefully.
- The introduction of ethnic monitoring to assist in analysis services, employment opportunities and research needs in respect of special issues of concern.
- Information to be translated into appropriate minority ethnic languages, pictorial information and ideas to be introduced to ensure information is reaching those who are illiterate in English and in their mother tongue.
- All training on the Children Act to integrate anti-racist, anti-discriminatory approach throughout its activities.
- Local authorities, health authorities and voluntary agencies must take into account the diversity of needs from within the Asian community when assessing priorities for community care and personal social services.

The NHS and Community Care Act 1990

The NHS and Community Care Act 1990 which is being phased in over a period of time is another important piece of legislation which will have significant implications for service provision to the Asian community.

The main points of concern are very similar to the Children Act and regard the following

- issues of language and communication;
- consultation;
- provision assessment and evaluation of services to the minority ethnic communities.

Local authorities cannot be sure that their services are free from racial discrimination and appropriate, adequate and accessible to minority ethnic groups unless they consult fully about services to be provided, amass what is provided and evaluate their effectiveness in conjunction with the local communities.

In November 1989, the White Paper entitled *Caring for People, Community Care in the Next Decade and Beyond* was published. Paragraph 2.9 states 'The government recognises that people from different backgrounds may have particular care needs and problems. Minority communities may have different concepts of community care and it is important that service providers are sensitive to these variations. Good community care will take account of the circumstances of minority communities and will be planned in consultation with them'.

Although there is a positive commitment to take account of minority ethnic needs with the community care plan, there is still much to be done to reflect this commitment as a reality. The Community Care Act is set to pose a whole number of issues for service providers; faced with inadequate resources and spasmodic information about its implementation, the climate is tense.

All community care plans are required to acknowledge the presence of Black and minority ethnic peoples within their authority, and devise packages of care which are sensitive and appropriate to their needs. It is important that the Act includes references to individuals' racial, cultural, religious and linguistic needs in areas such as assessment, case management, training, mental illness, purchasing, contracting, budgeting and monitoring.

Changes in community care – the implications for Black, and minority ethnic communities

Below are extracts taken from a meeting entitled *Agenda for Action* organised by the community care project of the National Council for Voluntary Organisations and the Race Equality Unit. It is not the intention of this chapter to give a detailed account of the implications of the Community Care Act for Black and Asian communities; what will be described are the major points to address in establishing a coherent framework to implement the changes in community care constructing and approaching so that they meet the needs of the users from minority ethnic communities adequately.

The model for good practice in the Children Act section of this chapter will also be helpful in considering positive ways for action in implementing community care plans.

Major points for consideration

- The government has not defined social care. Social care should not be compartmentalised or stereotyped, but should be seen as action taken to enhance the quality of life of people with all kinds of disability and long-term ill health. In each ethnic group, different cultural factors apply, and this must be reflected in the range of services available to support people.
- Black voluntary organisations have a more holistic approach to meeting needs than many White voluntary and statutory organisations. They generally provide a varied range of different services under one roof. This is a positive strength, not as is often assumed, a lack of professionalism.
- Local authorities, which will be responsible for planning and coordinating services, must consult fully with Black and minority ethnic communities. Such consultation must involve Black users and carers, as well as service-providing groups, and it must be real – not window dressing. The results of the consultation must be reflected in the decisions made and in the way resources are allocated – and this should be monitored.
- Local authorities will be responsible for assessing the needs of individuals. The criteria against which people are assessed must be anti-racist and arrived at in consultation with different Black communities. The people who carry out assessment should have appropriate knowledge and experience, and there should be a right of appeal.
- The government says carers should be supported. The needs of Black carers have been overlooked, partly because of the myths about extended families and their capacity to care for all members. Black carers desperately need information and access to appropriate services – and should be fully consulted on their needs.
- The government is urging local authorities to develop contracts with the private and voluntary sectors to provide services. Resources for community care are at present monopolised by White communities and White voluntary organisations. New kinds of services are needed by Black people, and Black voluntary organisations may be in a position to supply those. But for this to happen, Black people need to be involved in awarding and in monitoring contracts; Black organisations need more information about the implications of contracts; and they will need support to develop services. The 'enabling role' of local authorities should

include such support, but local authorities will have to be much more responsive than they are at present to convince voluntary groups that they are genuinely seeking to enable rather than exploit Black groups. Contracts are not the answer to everything, and grant aid should continue and become available to Black groups.

The government should issue clear guidance to local authorities on consulting Black communities about social care needs and ensuring that appropriate services exist. Any national monitoring of the quantity and quality of community care should include Black representation and take into account the duty placed on local authorities in the Race Relations Act to provide for the needs for *all* sections of the community.

Signpost

In addressing the needs of the black community, there are a number of strategies which may be used and developed to perpetuate a more comprehensive and sensitive service delivery. The recommendations listed in this chapter are by no means exhaustive; they simply offer suggestions to redress inequalities across all services and practice. Current changes in legislation regarding minority ethnic communities are moving closer to bridging the gap between Black service users and White service providers. The Children Act 1989 and the NHS Community Care Act 1990 will take important steps in developing an integrated caring service which is anti-discriminatory and anti-racist. The extent of their usefulness will depend upon the level of commitment of the reader to challenge their organisation. Although we are fortunate to have legislation which will help us to do this, there is little knowledge of them and the context in which they may be implemented. Inevitably, there will never be an end or a conclusion: both will be pending and relative to changes within the economic, social and political framework. It will always be necessary to place the Black community on a high profile, despite pressures of financial and practical resources. Credibility is demonstrated through plans of action, determined to adhere to anti-racist and anti-discriminatory policies, if they fall from one to 10 on the agenda, the struggle would have been for nothing and will be detrimental not only to the Black community, but also to professionals who have worked so hard to maintain good practice.

7. An update of new legislation and its impact on working in partnership

Much has been written and documented on service provision to children with learning disabilities in Asian families. Many agencies have raised their concern about the need to develop and improve services to this target group. However, there remains work to be done on developing cohesive multi-agency strategies which can address the needs of the whole child in collaboration with parents, voluntary organisations, statutory organisations and the children themselves.

Chapters 5 and 6 go some way in addressing the need for agencies to build in the new aspects of legislation such as the Children Act 1989 and the NHS Community Care Act 1990, and their implications for services to the Asian parents with a disabled child. The information written in these chapters is transferable to various contexts, particularly where building up links with the Asian community and methods of consultation are concerned.

It is not the intention of this chapter to provide detailed analysis of current changes in legislation such as the 1993 Education Act or the guidance on community child health services (Department of Health, 1995) and their impact on services to Asian parents with a disabled child. *An Agenda for Action* (National Children's Bureau, 1994) covers these points.

What will be discussed is the need to develop strategic procedures which identify key elements of concern for Asian parents; including references to race, language needs, religion and culture.

Particular emphasis will be made on the lack of information and knowledge of minority communities held by health service purchasers and providers, especially in the context of the new power of purchasers in the form of GP fund-holders.

Child Health Issues

The NHS has undergone many changes as a result of the NHS and Community Care Act 1990, none more so than the role of purchaser and provider and the absence of providing qualitative services which integrate equality issues.

To achieve equality in service provision it has to be acknowledged as a key principle worth achieving. While there may be a great willingness among health service managers to do this they are not always sure about how to proceed. The real question is how they interpret issues which affect minority ethnic communities and how this should be linked into auditing arrangements and purchaser–provider contracts.

Sadly, where there is a lack of knowledge of the real issues and how they affect Asian communities, contracts do not make specific reference to these needs and the result is poor service provision and therefore a poor quality of life for this target group.

It is absolutely imperative that there is acknowledged reference to the health needs of minority ethnic populations in all service contracts and that detailed audit reviews are undertaken to inform purchasers and providers of areas of need.

In defining the principles of good child health services we need to consider what Asian families want – this begins the question about good consultation and improving access to information about their children, and of course the valuable informative role that parents can play.

Beginning the Process

Purchasers should ensure that their child health needs assessment process identifies the specific needs of the local Asian community. This can then be used to set clear targets, inform providers about the development of contracts and monitor service impact against demographic information.

Similarly, providers should develop systems and procedures to monitor patterns of activity, indicators of health needs and outcomes of care by ethnicity. Particular attention should be made on utilising information from the 1991 Census to inform service development and provision to the Asian community.

In both contexts it is evident that there is a need to develop a strategy for active community participation in service planning and review. This entails a wider framework for involving Asian parents, users, carers and communities in continuing processes of agenda setting and decision making.

The management executive's *Local Voices* document (NHS Management Executive, 1992) provides guidance and encourages health authorities to develop a clear communication strategy with their local populations, as part of this it is important to include the participation of black populations.

Asian parents need to be involved in the dialogue which identifies specific services to meet the individual needs of their child, one way to ensure this takes place is to encourage Asian parents to take part in the commissioning process. Furthermore it is important when negotiating contracts for services that purchasers such as GP fundholders should satisfy themselves that provider units have established mechanisms which enable Asian parents, carers and users to express their views and levels of satisfaction with service delivery.

This must also incorporate methods of participation which are appropriate to the diversity of the issues consulted on and the experiences and needs of Asian parents and their child.

Ethnic record keeping and monitoring in service provision can be a very valuable tool to enable the process of planning and review to reflect the specific health care needs of the Asian population which can be formally linked to quality assurance and customer care programmes. Medical audits can also be used, to include the analysis of treatment decisions and clinical outcomes.

The 1993 Education Act states that DHAs must ensure that their purchasing arrangements take account of their responsibility to contribute to the identification and assessment of children with special educational needs. This involves the appointment of a designated medical officer to coordinate information and assessments.

The Citizens Charter has evoked immense activity in the health authorities to establish effective ways of working with local communities to determine how assessments should take place and what kind of support is needed. With reference to the medical role in educational assessment and the Asian community a number of issues have been raised. These mostly centre around parents' lack of knowledge about the changes in the 1993 Education Act and the role of the health service in addition to how Asian parents perceive themselves within these changes – especially how to acknowledge that they really do have a say in any assessment that is carried out on their child.

Language issues obviously exacerbate the difficulties, as do unfamiliarity with the protocols of entering into any discussion about their child.

Furthermore Asian parents who do experience language difficulties are far more vulnerable in the maze of medical diagnosis. How can they provide an informed opinion about the medical/educational assessment of their child if they do not fully understand the diagnosis?

Assessment is a key area which has an impact across all services, its facility is to provide a clear picture of the child's needs to ensure appropriate service intervention. No matter what the situation, whether it be an assessment for social services or health or education, there is still no clear strategy for integrating ethnicity, culture, religion and language.

Below is a framework which can be used to suggest how health authorities, education and social services departments can improve their assessment methods.

Key principles for assessment

- acknowledge that in-house assessment procedures may not address the child's needs in terms of ethnicity, culture, language and religion;
- recognise that staff may feel unskilled about asking questions about ethnicity and culture to the extent that they do not ask them;
- identify support mechanisms for staff to overcome these anxieties through staff development programmes – for example, by training;
- be clear and honest in your approach to the assessment of cultural needs, do not assume all Asian children are the same;
- it is not helpful to ask questions (such as: 'what is your culture?') that you would never ask of a white child;
- think about the information you need to inform the assessment and ask questions around that for example – what food do you enjoy eating, are there any special days in the year, what do you like to wear, who do you like to play with?
- Are there questions which may be offensive? It is important to understand that there may be some words which are culturally

inappropriate, for example parts of the body. This can have major implications for assessments on child abuse, and will require special attention to language;

- in developing behaviour modification programmes, consider the implications for particular social/personal skills: are they culturally sensitive and religiously appropriate? For example, it is religiously unacceptable and culturally inappropriate for Muslim girls to shake men's hands as a form of greeting. If this is encouraged as part of a behaviour programme it would not be reinforced in the home;
- develop assessments in consultation with the parents of the child, involve them at all stages and encourage them to participate as a legitimate right;
- be aware of your own assumptions and challenge these wherever you can, remember you are not responding to 'special needs' but to the individual need of the child.

Changes introduced through the *1993 Education Act and the Code of Practice* (Department for Education, 1994) now give new responsibilities to social service departments, the LEA and schools to work together in the statutory and the school-based stages of assessment. This has meant that many schools and LEAs are having to address their school policies and plans, to incorporate the needs of Asian parents. Issues of consultation with the local Asian community about support for parents, access to bilingual services such as professional interpreters, translators and advocates, are just some of the areas being investigated to enable LEAs to identify 'named persons', that is a person chosen by the LEA, with the help of parents, to give information and advice about the child's special educational needs. A named person can be a friend of the family or a member of a voluntary organisation.

Again, this requires special attention to mobilise the Asian community to work in partnership with the LEA and schools. Asian parents need to know how they can be helped in the assessment process, how they can nominate 'named persons' and how parents can be supported if they disagree with the way the system works. For example, Asian parents now need support in accessing the new Special Educational Needs Tribunals and many schools will need additional support in ensuring that school policies on special educational needs address the additional special needs of the Asian community.

Issues for Parents

LEAs and schools will need to consider how the new arrangements for school-based and statutory assessment (and their related review arrangements) will appear to parents from the Asian community. For example, parents may require information on the following issues:

- What is an assessment and how does the process work?
- How does this process affect my child?
- What is my role as a parent, how can I articulate the needs of my child?
- What is the purpose of a statement?
- Can I choose which school my child can go to?
- I thought professionals have all the answers – what can they expect from me?
- What is the role of the named person?
- What is a Special Educational Needs Tribunal, what happens if I disagree – will they send my child back home?
- The list is by no means conclusive and the questions asked here are not peculiar to Asian parents but to all parents: what is different is the response to them by LEAs and schools.

A Response by LEAs and Schools

Acknowledging the role of schools and the LEA to present information about special educational needs and assessment in a meaningful way by:

- providing information in community languages. The DFE's guide for parents is a useful starting point and is available in minority ethnic languages;
- working in consultation with parent groups set up in the schools to address parents needs, anxieties and concerns about the assessment process;
- appointing bilingual support staff to facilitate the process of communication;
- running community-based workshops with bilingual workers and professional interpreters, to inform Asian parents and the Asian community about the functions of a 'named person';
- working with the health authority and social service departments to promote activities around promotion and publicity of the

assessment procedure and to identify and share models of good practice;

- defining the role and responsibility of schools with reference to school policies on educational needs, in particular arrangements for partnerships with parents, allocation of resources utilising outside support services and agencies, and in-service training of staff on equality issues;
- utilising minority ethnic media: radio, television and newspapers to inform the Asian community about statementing, assessments and partnership with parents;
- explaining professional terminology in community languages with follow-up support when needed;
- personal development workshops for parents, helping them to be assertive, challenging and confident;
- advice and support for parents to enable them to identify the early warning stages which may indicate that further advice is required.

It is apparent that all of the above is dependent on clear constructive consultation mechanisms which will be integral to any assessment or partnership process. Consultation is a buzz word of the 90s, sometimes used synonymously with communication and participation.

For consultation to be meaningful when working with the Asian community it would be advisable to ensure that information is jargon-free, that parents are given roles of status and are rewarded for their contributions, that parents are encouraged to ask questions and that resources are made available for interpreters, translators, transport. At this point, it will be helpful to refer to the models of good practice and implications for practitioners presented in Chapter 6.

Early Identification/Interpretation/Surveillance

It is a sad fact that cases of Asian children with disabilities are under-reported and sometimes undetected by parents. There is a huge gap in the system of diagnosis and early identification which has meant that many children's development has been further hindered because appropriate intervention had not been accessed due to parents' inability to identify abnormality in the early stages of child development. However, the health services, in particular health visitors, are also accountable here to some extent, for failing to ensure that where their investigation identifies peculiarities in the child's development that they need to inform parents of the long-term implications.

Again language issues may play a role and therefore it is essential that any information given is followed up to ensure that parents have understood what is happening with their child and are therefore clear about their position.

Many GP fund-holders are now carrying out surveillance programmes instead of the DHA, so they should be sure to integrate language issues and cultural mores which may affect the results of any surveillance programme that they develop. GPs should consult with community organisations and accept assistance from projects such as the Parent Advisor Project in Tower Hamlets and the Department of Health Mother and Baby Groups, as well as the document *Physical and Mental Handicap in the Asian Community: Can My Child Be Helped?* (National Children's Bureau, 1989). Information and resources in this area are definitely lacking, perhaps this in itself can justify pressure on purchasers to ask providers to tender for a contract which will research further into this area and produce some practice guidelines and/or a video.

Multi-disciplinary Assessment

There are a number of disciplines working together throughout the life of a child who is disabled. There is emphasis on joint working and the importance of showing models of good practice which effectively address race and culture. Equally there is a gradual progression to producing multi-disciplinary assessments which enable services for children to be more effective, less time-consuming and to work towards a better quality of life.

Unfortunately where race, culture and language needs are concerned some agencies do not work collectively, or are less advanced than others in integrating issues around the special individual needs of Asian children.

This is particularly evident at the time of notification/disclosure to parents of a child with severe learning disabilities, or a medical condition.

The messages from SCOPE's report *Right from the Start* (1994) and the North West Regional Health Authority report *Sharing the*

News (1992), have established the need to support parents through the process of disclosure and beyond. They have identified in great detail the anxieties that parents experience and the difficulty in coping. These reports are good examples of multidisciplinary working but they still have much to achieve in identifying key ways for health authorities to work where there are language and cultural barriers which must be overcome. It is at the point of diagnosis that Asian parents need the most support. If they are not given appropriate advice and counselling or if they miss out on early intervention support this will inevitably be to the detriment of the future welfare of the child. If there is ever an area which demonstrates unmet needs it is here: language issues are very profound in this situation and purchasers should allocate more resources into bilingual services such as link-worker schemes or professional interpreters.

Many Asian parents suffer immensely during the primary crisis stage of disclosure. This is further reinforced throughout the secondary and later stages of their child's life. The result of not having English as their mother tongue denies them access to support services and the help these services can obviously give them. They clearly require assistance in the form of culturally appropriate counselling, consistent advice and support and someone to talk to! Services must be restructured to improve the inadequate resourcing at this point, enabling Asian parents to become more aware of their child's needs and become more informed about the implications of their child's diagnosis for the future. It will assist future assessments of their child because the ground-work would have been done. Other disciplines therefore do not have to waste time re-covering lost ground or identifying unmet needs as hopefully much of this will have been established.

Child Health Records

The publication of guidance, *The Welfare of Children and Young People in Hospital* (HMSO, 1991), has been followed by parallel guidance on community child health services. It is anticipated that there will be a strong push towards parent-held child health records, giving parents more rights and empowering them in a similar way to the Children Act 1989. This has meant that parents will not only have more access to their child's records, but will be in an informed position to put forward questions to professionals and seek clarification on items they do not understand.

For Asian parents real empowerment lies in the system of communication and whether their language needs are addressed. Health visitors especially will have a crucial role to play here, as they will be in the best position to advise parents who have language needs about how important it is to access their child's health records and the best way to achieve this. It would be helpful if health visitors were able to identify those parents who have prospective language difficulties to purchasers and providers such as GPs and community nurses, so that adequate resources, for example interpreters, could be made available.

Child Protection Issues

The NSPCC and the Department of Health recently published the *ABCD Training Pack on Abuse and Children who are Disabled* (1993). It was the first time that training materials were produced which explored the issues for child protection workers and disability workers when addressing the increasing number of disabled children who are abused. There is also a growing debate about how treatment methods of control are abusive in themselves.

With reference to ethnicity and culture, the debate raises questions about how child protection procedures are seen to work against the child rather than for him/her. This is because the current legislation and assessment process fails to take account of religious and cultural child-rearing practices which need to be understood together with implications for marriage, guilt and shame in the community in context. There are also language issues and the difficulty of translating and/or repeating taboo sexual words.

The debate goes further to suggest that child protection must consider issues of system abuse or racial abuse which can reinforce and emphasise how agencies fail to meet the needs of Asian children with learning disabilities.

The Children Act 1989 states very clearly the need to identify the importance and interplay of ethnicity, religion, culture and language in assessing the needs of the child.

However, the child is a child first and he or she will be the best judge in determining how these factors affect his or her life.

Ethnicity Religion Culture Language	Non-disabled Child	Disabled Child	Child who has been able-bodied

All of the above will define different boundaries for working with the child and parents, one needs to investigate how these boundaries are set and to what extent they treat the child as a whole.

Furthermore children's and parents' views about abuse and how they perceive it is not always accounted for in professional definitions of abuse. While child protection may seek to identify abuse in categories of neglect, physical abuse, sexual abuse and emotional abuse, there is no category for racial abuse.

Black children suffer racism everyday in their lives, it is part of their experience of life and often has very devastating effects on a child's psychological well-being. This needs to be acknowledged in the standard definition of emotional abuse or appear as a category in its own right.

The UN Convention on the Rights of the Child

The Health of the Nation initiative and the Citizens' Charter have established the need to provide greater support for children within their own families and improved access to appropriate community based services. With reference to general health promotion and immunisation programmes, children with disabilities often miss out. In the case of many Asian children, because of the language difficulties they or their parents may experience, access is further denied.

In fact within the whole area of generic health care, communication is a powerful tool. It brings access to information, improved knowledge of services and empowerment to children. These are messages that are considered in the principles of the UN Convention on the Rights of the Child, namely:

- the need to respect the rights and responsibilities of parents and guardians in assisting them in bringing up their children;
- the child's right to privacy and confidentiality;
- to ensure that there is recognition of the child's rights to express views about his or her own health and treatment and to have those views taken into account according to age and maturity;

- to ensure that the child's best interests are the primary concern in making any decision;
- to ensure that all services and facilities provided for children conform to the standards of safety, staffing and supervision established by competent authorities;
- to ensure that all examinations and treatments are necessary and in the best interests of the child and do not interfere with the child's right to physical and personal integrity.

All of the above are excellent guides to set our standards against to improve children's services; for Asian children their effectiveness will be judged on how these services respond to their needs in respect of ethnicity, culture, religion and language needs and to their individual needs.

Children 'looked after' by the Local Authority

Children who are accommodated in short-term care schemes are accounted for in the above term 'looked after'. The Department of Health has revised the assessment and review forms for 'looked after' children by the local authority and for the first time these revised forms will have a specific disability focus. This means that some Asian families will be discussing medical or disability issues in the course of child care planning. In the light of what has been said already in Chapter 6 in the section under the Children Act 1989, there are specific duties for health authorities towards children staying or living away from home which require them to be sensitive and responsive to the following areas:

- the young persons perception of his or her health needs or disability;
- the rationale for any treatment;
- the implications of care upon the lives of the family;
- the management of treatment or medication within the care setting;
- any special areas of concern like sexuality, substance abuse, mental health problems, HIV infection (where confidentiality may be a major issue);
- counselling – for example on the implications of a condition like muscular dystrophy which will probably only impact on everyday life in early adolescence;

- the provision of aids and equipment;
- purchasing arrangements for specialist health care when a child or young person is placed out of his or her health authority of origin;
- management of any primary medical care required or provision of therapy;
- the interplay of ethnicity, religion, culture and language and how this impacts on all of the above.

Appropriate children's services can only be provided if each agency is fully informed about the nature of the community it is serving. Britain is now a multi-cultural, multi-religious and multi-lingual society: this has to be acknowledged before any effective strategy can be developed.

In this new age of the purchaser/provider split there are some key messages regarding health to be taken from the national guidelines, for example addressing the health needs of minority ethnic communities by targeting particular services, negotiating with providers to incorporate local targets in contracts and implementing ethnic monitoring.

The clinical audit is becoming a more powerful tool for looking at what kind of care children with disabilities are getting and how this can be improved. For example, ethnic monitoring could provide objective measures of access to services and identify the clinical appropriateness of different ethnic minority communities.

Notes for Purchasers/Providers

In the light of the Health of the Nation targets this means that there should be clear reference to action, planning targets and objectives for services to minority ethnic communities. For example:

- new quality standards relating to black and minority ethnic communities should be monitored and developed with black voluntary organisations;
- quality standards relating to the treatment of Asian children with disabilities should be improved through the involvement of parents, self-help groups and voluntary organisations;
- quality standards should include respect for privacy, dignity, religious and cultural beliefs. *Welfare of Children and Young People in Hospital* (HMSO, 1991) states that hospitals should consult with minority ethnic communities (see Chapter 6) to ensure their special needs are addressed appropriately;

- all patients and staff should be made aware of any bilingual services and how to gain access to the services provided;
- visiting arrangements and pastoral care in hospitals should be sensitive to the needs of all religions and cultures;
- all patients should receive the appropriate relevant diet;
- local arrangements should be made to ensure access to services by anyone, including children with special needs from minority ethnic communities;
- services and staff training programmes should recognise the need to be sensitive and remain appropriate to the special needs found within the local population.

The new DoH guidance on community child health services (1995) and the DFE Code of Practice (1994) on the identification and assessment of special educational needs have introduced more positive measures of working together to improve the quality of services for all children who are disabled. The issues for purchasers are many where Asian children who are disabled is concerned. This chapter has gone some way towards highlighting those.

There is much to be gained from joint working both within and across agencies and with parents. The school health service plays an instrumental role in early identification of special needs and purchasers should perceive their role as valuable in the assessment process. Similarly Asian parents themselves need to be encouraged to participate in this process, to articulate their concerns and identify the individual needs of their child.

Signpost

In addressing the needs of Asian children with disabilities there are a number of strategies which can be developed to establish more comprehensive services that are sensitive and appropriate to the child's background which take account of ethnicity and culture as part of the whole assessment of the child's needs.

Although we are now fortunate to have new legislation which will enable us to achieve this, there is little knowledge of its implications for Asian children and the context in which it might be implemented.

How can we progress? Which tools can we use to help us through the process of change? Research is a valuable tool and should be an integral part of service assessment to children from the Asian community. Social, economic and environmental factors should be identified rather than relying on over-generalised ethnic differences.

Professional interpreting and translation services should be provided with attention given to proper training for staff, in order to avoid a clash of expectations.

Due to the link between appropriate service provision and communication on the one hand and low uptake of services on the other, all purchasers/providers should evaluate the effectiveness of existing services in the context of recent legislation. These include the 1993 Education Act, the Code of Practice, and Department of Health guidance on community child health services.

Campaigns can be conducted with outreach workers and community-based teams to inform Asian parents about the legislation and how it affects them and their children. Special efforts should be made to disseminate information through the minority ethnic press and organisations to highlight particular issues and inform communities about particular services and of their need to participate.

Ethnic monitoring can be introduced to assist in the analysis of services, employment, parents' level of satisfaction with child care services.

Information should be translated into minority languages, though this is not a comprehensive solution because there are some Asian parents who are illiterate in their mother tongue and this issue too needs to be addressed.

Training should be provided to enable staff to manage change in the way that they provide services to the Asian community. Good professional practice is about how we develop our skills and knowledge, in order to be more responsive to the needs of Asian children with whom we may have contact. It is not about feeling de-skilled, de-motivated or lacking confidence, although some professionals experience these feelings.

The important message to remember is the commitment to provide equality in all services – a commitment measured by improving access, communication and active participation with parents and children from minority communities.

The real challenge is identifying the starting point, thinking through the issues and setting clear targets with achievable goals.

Below is an example of a model framework. It is suggested as a guide only but may be useful in working through those many 'bones of contention' that we need to discuss in some systematic way both at an organisational level and on a personal level.

The discussion and debate around planning and improving services to Asian children with disabilities is important. Everyone's contribution is valuable. Organisations need to establish their definitions on equality of care which are clear, meaningful and understood by everyone. Only then can the process move forward – and only then can we have good services which match equality with quality.

A Model Framework

Know where you're starting from	*Analyse:* • Strengths/obstacles • Philosophy and culture • Current standards of practice • Theories/ideologies used • Other factors/changes
Create shared agreement and ownership	• Changes needed • Philosophy needed • Shared definitions • Ownership through participation • Acceptable practice? • Address problems openly • Reward success
Set objectives	• Agree objectives • Communicate them widely • Identify priorities
Take action	• Clarify specific tasks • Standards of practice desired • Delegate responsibility • Agree methods • Set targets/deadlines
Evaluation	• Regular review of progress

Appendix 1 The questionnaire

For general information

Name of child

Parents name

Date of birth   Ethnicity   Religion

Medical history

....

....

....

Description of mental disability

Does child suffer from any physical disability?

General information

Section A **Attitudes of parent to child**

1. What does having a disabled child mean to you?

2. How do you feel other people see you as parents of a disabled child?

3. Do you feel that only you must be responsible for the welfare of your child?

4. How have you prepared for the future of your child. Do you encourage your child to learn basic skills which will help him/her cope with life without you?

5. How does the rest of the family react to your child?

6. Who is responsible for caring for the child?

7. Who makes the decisions about the child's needs?

Section B **Attitudes of parents to social workers**

8. Do you have a social worker?

9. Do you have problems explaining what you want to a social worker. Why?

10. Do you think that social workers care about your problems?

11. If you have a social worker how often do you see him/her?

12. Would you like to have a social worker?

Section C **Knowledge of services**

13. When you knew that your child was disabled who did you go to for help?

14. Was support offered to you, if yes, then by whom?

15. Do you know where the Social Services Area Office is located?

16. Do you know who to contact there or what the telephone number is?

17. Are you aware of the services available to you?

18. What services do you think you should have available to you?

19. When you need help who do you go to and what is the response?

20. Do you understand why your child needs to attend a special school?

21. What do you think about short-term care?

22. What do you think about fostering?

23. If you think fostering is a good idea would you prefer that your child be looked after by someone of the same culture and religion?

24. Do you know what short-term and long-term care means?

25. Do you understand what is meant by fostering?

26. Do you know what summer play schemes are?

27. Do you think the play schemes are a good idea?

Section D **General**

28. Do you believe the social workers have no understanding of your culture: beliefs and values?

29. Is communication your greatest difficulty?

30. Would you like to have more information about services available to you translated into your own language, why?

31. Would you like to meet other families who have a disabled child?

32. Would you like to have regular advice and counselling about services available?

33. Would you prefer that your child be kept away from children who do not have a disability?

34. Would you be interested in attending an open day at the social services department where you can discuss the welfare of your child?

35. Do you feel reluctant to take up services because your immigration status may be questioned?

36. What do you think about social services in general?

37. Do you receive any of the following benefits:
    (a) attendance allowance;
    (b) mobility allowance;
    (c) non-contributory invalidity pension (NCIP);
    (d) income support;
    (e) heating, laundry, clothing allowance, free school meals?

38. Are you satisfied with the education provided at your child's special school?

39. Any other information you wish to share about the needs of your child?

Appendix 2 Results of the questionnaire

Results of the questionnaire

The total number of respondents in this study was 35.

The study was initiated in 1986/87 with families from Manchester, and then in 1988 a further study was conducted to include families from Birmingham. Many of the families were contacted through the formal networking of Manchester Social Services and Birmingham Social Services. However, a few of the families were referred by members of the community or voluntary agencies.

The study was first piloted in Manchester and then after interviewing families in Birmingham, re-interviews took place with the parents in Manchester.

The data was collected using a questionnaire and semi-structured interview schedules.

The findings were made up of both soft and hard data and I have tried to record the results to demonstrate this.

Total number of respondents: No.=35

Section A	*Attitude of parent to child*	
What does having a disabled child mean to you?	Frustration/sadness 95%	Nothing 5%

	Ignore	Sympathetic	Unsympathetic
How do you feel other people see you as parents of a disabled child?	18%	68%	14%

Do you feel only you should be responsible for the welfare of your child?	Yes 100%	No 0%	
Have you prepared for the future of your child?	Yes 60%	No 10%	Not really sure 30%
How does the rest of your family react to to your child?	Favourably 98%	No difference 2%	
Who is responsible for caring for your child?	Mum 12%	Dad 0%	Both 88%
Who makes the decisions about your child's needs?	Mum 0%	Dad 8%	Both 92%

Section B **Attitudes of parents to social workers**

Do you have a social worker?	Yes 78%	No 22%
Do you have problems explaining your needs to your social worker?	Yes 28%	No 72%
Do you think social workers care about your problems?	Yes 28%	No 72%
Would you like to have the help of a social worker?	Yes 100%	No 0%

Section C **Knowledge of services**

	GP	Community/ Friend	Social services	Other
When you knew your child was disabled who did you go to for help?	40%	45%	2%	13%
Was support offered to you?		Yes 100%	No 0%	

Do you know where the Social Services Area Office is?		Yes 38%		No 62%
Are you aware of the services available to you?		Yes 40%		No 60%
Do you understand why your child needs to attend special school?		Yes 83%		No 17%
What do you think about short-term care?	Good 20%	Bad 2%	Don't know 78%	
Do you know what short-term care is?	Yes 20%	No 80%		
If you think fostering is a good idea would you prefer your child to be looked after by someone of same culture and religion?	Yes 80%	No 0%	Don't mind 20%	
Do you know what summer play schemes are?	Yes 60%		No 40%	
Do you think they are a good idea?	Yes 80%		No 20%	

Section D General questions

Do you think social workers have no understanding of your culture and belief values?		Yes 88%		No 12%

Is communication a great difficulty?	Yes 88%	No 12%
Would you like to meet other families who have a disabled child?	Yes 98%	No 2%
Would you like to have regular advice and counselling?	Yes 100%	No 0%

References and suggested further reading

ABCD Consortium (1993) *The ABCD Pack: Abuse and Children who are Disabled*. NSPCC/Chailey Heritage/National Deaf Children's Society/Way Ahead Consultancy.

Barker, J (1984) *Black and Asian Old People in Britain*. Age Concern Race Research Unit.

Bundley, S and others, 'Race, consanguinity and social features in Birmingham babies, a basis for prospective study', *Journal of Epidemiology and Community Health*, Vol. 44, No. 2, pp130–135.

Burghart, R (1988) 'The Use of Cultural Knowledge in the Provision of Health Care Services among Ethnic Minorities in Britain: the Care of Residents and Citizens of South Asian Origin *in* Allen, S and Macey, M (eds) *Race and Social Policy*, ESRC.

Council for Disabled Children (1994) *An Agenda for Action: a handbook to support the implementation of the special educational needs arrangements in the Education Act 1993*. National Children's Bureau.

Council for Disabled Children (1995) *Help Starts Here: a guide for parents of children with special needs*. 3rd ed. National Children's Bureau.

Davis, H and Russell, R (1989) *Physical and Mental Handicap in the Asian Community: Can My Child Be Helped?: Video Support Material*. National Children's Bureau.

Department for Education (1994) *Code of Practice on the Identification and Assessment of Special Educational Needs*. The Department for Education.

Department for Education (1994) *Special Educational Needs: a guide for parents*. The Department for Education.

Department of Health (1991) *The Welfare of Children and Young People in Hospital*. HMSO.

Department of Health (1995) *Child Health in the Community: a guide to good practice.* The Department of Health.

Duncan, DM ed. (1988) *Working with Bi-lingual Language Disability.* Croom Helm.

Gunaratnam, Y (1993) *Checklist: Health and Race: A Starting Point for Managers on Improving Services for Black Populations.* Kings Fund Centre.

Henley, A (1979) *Asian Patients in Hospital and at Home.* King Edward's Hospital Fund for London.

Jupp, TC and Davies, E (1974) *The Background and Employment of Asian Immigrants: a manual for preparing short courses, talks and discussions.* Runnymede Trust.

Karseras, P and Hopkins, E (1987) *Britain's Asians: Health in the Community.* Wiley.

Keebles, P (1984) *Disability in Minority Ethnic Groups: a factsheet of issues and initiatives.* RADAR.

Khan, A (1981) *Islamic Medicine.* Commission for Racial Equality.

Leonard, A (1994) *Right from the Start: looking at diagnosis and disclosure – parents describe how they found out about their child's disability.* SCOPE.

NHS Management Executive (1992) *Local Voices, the views of local people in purchasing for health.*

Newell, P (1988) *ACE Special Education Handbook.* College Hill Press.

Northwest Regional Advisory Group on Learning Disabilities (1992) *Sharing the News – a resource for developing guidelines for good practice procedures and training in informing parents of diagnosis of a child's impairment.* Northwest Regional Health Authority.

Pearson, M (1991) 'Ethnic Differences in Infant Health' *Archives of Disease in Childhood*: January.

Pearson, M (1988) *Black and Ethnic Minority Elders in Britain.* University of Keele.

Pocock, D (1975) *Understanding Social Anthropology.* Hodder and Stoughton.

Social Services Inspectorate (1994) *Services to Disabled Children and their Families: Report of the national inspection of services to disabled children and their families.* HMSO.

Teaching About India, Bangladesh and Pakistan (1976) *in Education and Community Relations.* Commission for Racial Equality.

Index

INDEX 113